TRAIN SMART

SMART

Perfect Trainings Every Time

TRAIN SMART

Perfect Trainings Every Time

Rich Allen, Ph.D.

The Brain Store®, Inc.

TrainSmart: Perfect Trainings Every Time
By Rich Allen, Ph.D.

©2001 The Brain Store®, Inc.

Design: Tracy Linares
Developmental/Managing Editor: Karen Markowitz
Associate Editor: Gail Olson

Printed in the United States of America
Published by The Brain Store®, Inc.
San Diego, CA, USA

ISBN # 1-890460-10-9

All rights reserved. Written permission required from the publisher to use or reproduce any part of this book including the drawings, graphs, illustrations, or text except for brief quotations in critical reviews or articles.

For additional copies or bulk discounts contact:

The Brain Store®, Inc.
4202 Sorrento Valley Blvd., #B
San Diego, CA 92121
Phone (858) 546-7555 • Fax (858) 546-7560
www.thebrainstore.com

Acknowledgments

Over the past two decades, I have had the opportunity to work with a number of extraordinarily gifted individuals. I am grateful that each of them has been such an important part of my professional life.

Rob Abernathy
Susan Adams
Carole Allen
Tim Andrews
Scott Bornstein
Laura Bowen
Linda Brown
Phil Bryson
Dr. Stephanie Burns
Micheal Carr
Peter Coldicott
Bobbi DePorter
David Edwards
Dr. Billie Enz
Dr. Donald J. Freeman
Judy Green
Sean Hall

Allison Helstrup
Jan Hensley
Pete LaGrego
John LeTellier
Dee Lindenberger
Dr. James McCray
Doug McBride
Dr. Cristal McGill
Jim Moore
Kate Neal
Bill Payne
Mark Reardon
Timothy Giles Rickett
Richard Scheaff
Sarah Singer-Nourie
Lance Tomlinson
Larry Wilson

In writing this book, two people have greatly contributed to the process and deserve *special thanks*: Dr. Cristal McGill for her thorough and tireless research assistance; Dee Lindenberger for her voluntary edits of several early manuscript versions. Finally, thanks to my family, Tara Allen; Howell Babbitt and Edwina Wolfrey; Joanne and Axel Neimer; Karen, Lauren, Ben, and Angela McCutcheon; and Barb and David Young.

Table of Contents

continued...

PART TWO *continued...*

PART THREE

From Plan to Applause 131

APPENDIX

Preface

This book represents a culmination of more than 20 years of study and practice as a professional trainer and teacher. I've found that no matter where I go in the world and no matter what age group I'm addressing, people almost always respond quickly and easily to learning sessions that incorporate the principles and concepts outlined in *TrainSmart*.

Simply stated, I'm now convinced that there are consistencies in language patterns, delivery styles, training plans, and "set designs" that successful trainers and educators tend to adopt. When these elements are orchestrated effectively, learning goals are achieved with maximum efficiency and impact.

The tie that binds these strategies together is the brain, but more specifically, how the brain naturally learns best—what causes it to remember, stay focused, think, get excited, shut down, and wake up! Although my own learning journey is far from complete, the time feels right for creating a compendium of techniques that emphasize training smarter, not harder. My hope is that you'll find yourself—novice and expert alike—ever closer to achieving maximum impact each time you step up onto the "stage."

Many of the techniques I currently use as a trainer were learned in my first career as an actor. Thus, concepts such as establishing mood, influencing states, voice projection, trust, surprise, and novelty are themes I've found to be common to both the theatre and the training room. Audiences respond extremely well to these techniques because the brain does not discriminate between entertainment and education. A teenager buzzing from the stimulation of a video game cannot help but remember the rules, characteristics, strategies, and tools inherent in the game, just as the patrons of a captivating theatrical performance can't help but follow every nuance of the play. Our brain thrives on such stimulation. In fact, this is learning at its best!

Although the TrainSmart principles and concepts presented in this book are simple and direct, incorporating them into your training routine may require some practice. However, it will be well worth the time spent.

When people are trained in a way that agrees with their instincts, they respond with enthusiasm, encores, and standing ovations. Although this may not necessarily be our primary goal, such results are a nice finale; don't you think? Most importantly, an audience's response provides us with a valuable gauge by which to assess and improve our effectiveness as trainers.

Whenever I interact with an audience, I receive valuable feedback and information that enhances my own learning. Therefore, please feel free to contact me via email should you wish to share any impressions or insights gleaned from your reading and implementation of the ideas. This book is ultimately dedicated to you, the educators and trainers of the world, who have been charged with the awesome responsibility of enlightening others. May you thrive in your work.

Let the show begin!

For Tara...
My continual source of inspiration!

All the world's a stage...
—William Shakespeare

Part One

Prepare for Perfect Trainings Every Time

Part One Preview

Overview

**The Five Pillars of the
TrainSmart Model**
Engage
Frame
Explore
Debrief
Reflect

**The Bricks and Mortar of the
TrainSmart Model**

The Bricks...
Teach People, Not Content
Awareness Leads to Choice
Learning + Enjoyment = Retention
Application Is Everything
Stories Are Great

...and Mortar
Crest of the Wave
Frames Create Meaning
Make it Memorable
Open Loops
Train Directly to the Point

Sample TrainSmart Schedule

Overview

Although a great deal of territory is covered in *TrainSmart*, you'll find that the principles are swiftly internalized because they're inherent to how the brain naturally learns best. Therefore, they should make *perfect sense* to you. Beyond this, they'll make *perfect sense* to your audience! And perhaps most importantly, everyone will learn more and experience greater joy in the process. Does this sound too good to be true? It's not! In fact, as you journey forth, you're likely to say to yourself, "this is too simple to be anything *but* true."

Part One introduces you to the TrainSmart approach—the pillars and foundation upon which the model is built. *Part Two* outlines the 25 Key Concepts that transform the model into practical applications for immediate implementation, and *Part Three* presents a handful of powerful parables that will linger in the minds of your learners long after your closing remarks. Finally, *TrainSmart* concludes with a checklist that ensures your trainings will hit the mark every time.

The ideas presented here are entirely consistent with concepts about effective learning techniques that some of the brightest minds in history have created. These once tiny seeds of thought, however, are now stately oaks of educational practice that have stood the test of time. From this rich ground of our collective consciousness has emerged a model that reflects the art and science of training smarter, not harder. Let's take a closer look.

The Five Pillars of the TrainSmart Model

The term *model* is defined here as "a preliminary construction that serves as a plan from which a final product is made." Thus, the following *model* for planning a perfect training can be customized according to the needs of your particular situation. In other words, the following paradigm represents a basic framework that requires your creativity, planning, and purposeful action to complete.

Once you have journeyed well into TrainSmart territory, you'll want to devise a practical plan for your very next training that incorporates what you've learned. The five pillars diagramed below represent the action steps of the model. You will want to ensure their presence in every training plan.

Of course, *how* and *when* you incorporate them is completely dependent upon your own personal style, objectives, environment, and experience. The goal is to become proficient in the use of the tools you're soon to possess while building upon the foundation of the TrainSmart model.

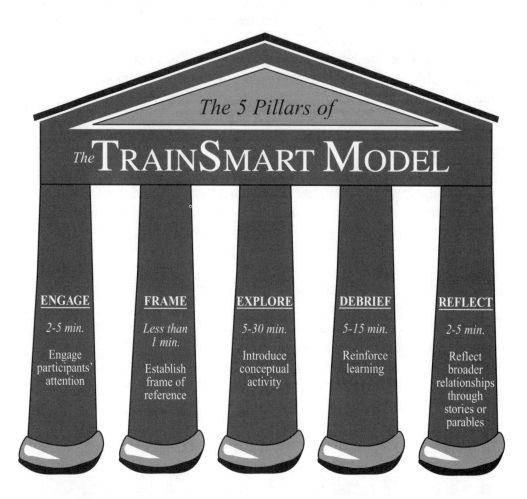

The 5 Pillars of

The TRAINSMART MODEL

ENGAGE	FRAME	EXPLORE	DEBRIEF	REFLECT
2-5 min.	*Less than 1 min.*	*5-30 min.*	*5-15 min.*	*2-5 min.*
Engage participants' attention	Establish frame of reference	Introduce conceptual activity	Reinforce learning	Reflect broader relationships through stories or parables

1. Engage

This step serves as an *energizer* and/or an *icebreaker* in certain situations. Its primary purpose, however, is to mentally prepare participants for the learning session ahead. The objectives are to actively bring participants into the moment, reduce the effect of any personal distractions and the anxiety of being in an unfamiliar setting, and to focus their brains.

2. Frame

This section of the model addresses participants' concerns while also explaining the trainer's immediate objective(s). Generally, questions such as the following float around in participants' mind until addressed: (1) Why am I here? (2) What am I supposed to learn? (3) How is this information important to me? And, (4) How will this new knowledge benefit me either personally or professionally?

3. Explore

This active phase is meant to introduce participants to the key content of your training—not by telling them about it, but by involving them in it. Good exploration activities involve sensory experiences and attention to a variety of learning styles and multiple intelligences. When participants are stimulated on multiple levels—physically, mentally, socially, and/or emotionally—comprehension and recall improve.

4. Debrief

The purpose of this phase is to highlight and reinforce the key points of your training. It is generally accomplished through the facilitation of participant dialogue and/or interaction that relates to the prior exploration activity. This step also gives trainers the opportunity to determine what content participants have internalized and where further elaboration is necessary. The key in this stage is to *guide* participants towards a clear understanding of the content.

5. Reflect

The reflection phase often incorporates a parable, personal example, or metaphor to illustrate the concept in a "real-life" context. The objective of this phase is to help participants identify the broader meaning of the content. Trainers often close with a reflection activity to leave learners with a deep and lasting impression of the material.

The real-life example on the following page illustrates what the TrainSmart model might look like when incorporated into a sales seminar for realtors:

A Real-Life Training Example

What:
A Sales Seminar for Realtors

Purpose:
Train New Realtors in the Art of Building Relationships with Customers

Action Steps:

Engage

Ask participants to pair up and simulate a situation in which they're meeting each other for the first time. Have the pairs decide which of them will play the part of the realtor and which the client. Either meet with the realtors briefly or pass a card to each of them explaining their specific role—that of a very rude salesperson. When the role-play gets underway, the client is baffled as she/he attempts to make a positive contact. This unexpected exercise gets everyone laughing and helps release the anxiety inherent in a new learning environment.

Frame

Flip a switch and project an overhead transparency on the screen that illustrates "The Anatomy of a Real Estate Sale." The diagram reflects the areas of content that will be covered in the training. Explain the value of the skill they are about to learn and how it will be of benefit to them.

Explore

After a brief explanation of the brainstorming process, divide the audience into small groups to brainstorm the essential elements of a successful first contact between a realtor and potential client. Ask a volunteer in each group to record the ideas generated by the group. Afterwards, have the groups share their responses with the entire class. Then ask for volunteer pairs to demonstrate a refined first contact for the class, this time incorporating as many positive elements as possible.

continued...

Debrief

As a follow-up to the exploration activity, ask the seated participants to evaluate the scene they've just observed. Provide guiding questions such as (1) What worked? (2) What didn't work? (3) Would you have done anything differently? (4) Would you have been impressed if you were the client? Then pose broader questions such as (5) Is there a single *correct* way to greet a new client? (6) What might you want to consider when sizing up the client and steering the interaction? Rather than *telling* them, *guide* participants towards the appropriate shifts in thinking.

Reflect

Write an astronomical sum up on the board. Explain that the figure represents how much money was lost in deals that fell through as a result of the groups' ineffective initial contacts. Then, distribute a synthetic million-dollar bill to each member of the group and say, "Now this reflects your subsequent financial success as a result of your newly perfected greeting skills." Conclude this part of the training with an account of a personal experience in which a friendly greeting you extended to a seatmate on a flight to Hawaii resulted in a 5-million-dollar sale or your own version of a related story.

The Bricks and Mortar
of the TrainSmart Model

This section introduces ten fundamental aspects of the TrainSmart approach to training. They are divided into two distinct sections. First, we'll look at five critical beliefs that comprise the building blocks of the model—the "bricks." Then we'll examine five guiding principles of effective training that hold it all together—the "mortar."

Your ability to clearly articulate your beliefs, thoughts, and opinions about what makes learning happen is an integral part of your training effectiveness. Such core beliefs represent the foundation upon which all of what you do as a trainer is built. It is important to recognize that each trainer brings to the table a different set of beliefs and perspectives that make her/him unique. They are strongly influenced by each person's diverse life experiences and influences. The following five beliefs represent the foundation of the TrainSmart model. Let's review them one brick at a time.

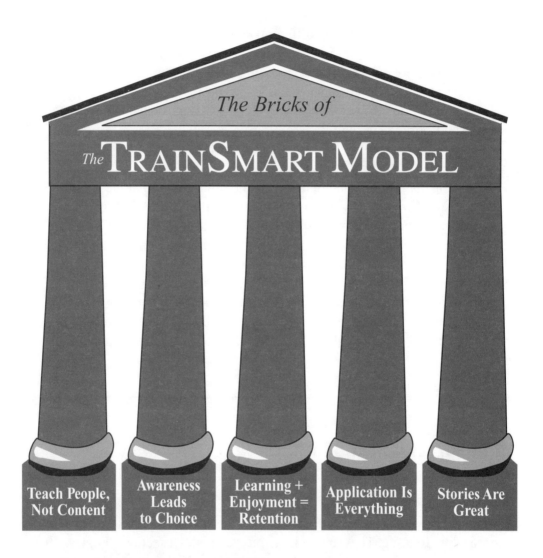

The Bricks of

The TRAINSMART MODEL

| Teach People, Not Content | Awareness Leads to Choice | Learning + Enjoyment = Retention | Application Is Everything | Stories Are Great |

1. Teach People, Not Content

Undeniably, content is important. After all, it's the primary reason why companies invest in seminars. The reality, however, is that *content* means very little outside of a *human* context. The TrainSmart approach recognizes this fact. Learners are, first and foremost, *people*, and *their* needs come first. Only when this is truly taken into account can real training begin.

While at first glance this core belief may sound elementary, its impact reaches far beyond what most trainers might initially imagine. Maintaining a focus on *people first* requires a basic shift in thinking. Another way of saying this is, don't teach *to* people, teach *with* them. Training *to* a group assumes that instruction happens only in one direction—from the trainer to the participants. Training *with* a group acknowledges that learning is bilateral and merely represents an exchange between individuals. This framework acknowledges that the trainer's point of view is *not* the *only* valid one. Ultimately, being sensitive to the needs of the group and respecting each individual will foster the type of safe and trusting environment that supports optimal learning.

2. Awareness Leads to Choice

People always make the best choice available to them. While this statement is not meant to open up a psychological or philosophical debate, it does underscore the importance of attending to the training *process*, as well as the *content*. If we want participants to use their head and make good decisions, we must provide the means for practicing these skills. Perhaps then, one of our roles as a trainer is to help learners become aware of more options, patterns, potentials, and possibilities.

Consider, for example, the metaphor of a lavish buffet featuring the best dishes of a renowned chef. Although the chef prepares dozens of exquisite dishes, diners choose what they'll taste. The goal of the trainer, like the chef, is to make the material as attractive and "edible" as possible. But ultimately, the learner, like the diner, will choose what to consume.

The common response to feeling cajoled or controlled is one of resentment, while the common response to being given choice and control is ownership and personal responsibility. Within this framework, the function of trainers is quite simple. Our primary purpose is to increase the number of options participants have in their choice bank. Although presenting learners with choices can result in the appearance of a somewhat "chaotic" setting, the mix of freedom and responsibility ultimately results in a more dynamic learning environment. People will always make their own choices, both in the seminar room and in life. As their awareness grows, however, their chance of success multiplies, as well.

3. Learning + Enjoyment = Retention

Cognitive scientists agree that emotions have a significant effect on our recall. Think about it: What do you remember from your own childhood? If you're like most people, your most durable memories fall into one of two distinct categories—times of great pleasure or great pain. As a trainer, the idea of deliberately using negative emotions to influence recall is beyond reason—unless, of course, you're a boot-camp drill sergeant. Connecting positive emotions, however, to content is clearly a reasonable and effective retention strategy.

There is no shortage of ways to enhance the emotional climate of a learning environment. But before we can incorporate them, we need to take an introspective look at our own attitudes with regard to humor, joy, and playful interaction within the training environment. A positive connection has not always been reinforced between these elements, especially in traditional settings. However, many of the factors that contribute to an effective training room—personal expression, human connection, meaningful interaction, a sense of emotional safety, mutual respect, etc.—are also the factors that contribute to a sense of personal enjoyment. There is a deep and powerful connection. Think back to your childhood again: Did you ever truly master anything that you didn't enjoy?

4. Application Is Everything

Learners need to make new knowledge applicable to their own unique situations. This concept applies across almost all arenas of instruction. Demonstrating the validity or usefulness of the knowledge through association with concrete examples and real-life encounters not only helps participants understand and apply the content, it also helps them remember it!

Nothing is taught if nothing is learned.
And nothing is learned if nothing is applied.

Small group exercises, games, case studies, brain twisters, and role-plays are all examples of ways participants might apply content to their lives. Perhaps, after you present a couple of key points, participants could divide into small groups and discuss how they might apply the content in their work or home life. Facilitating such interactions frequently would allow participants to build their understanding of how to use their new knowledge.

I sometimes open a lesson by posing a problem. I might say, "Please help me identify what's wrong with the following situation?" In this case, the application becomes the starting point of the presentation. Subsequently, variations on the problem are presented and ways to address it are discussed.

5. Stories Are Great

Long before there were books or movies or computers, there were stories—metaphorical tales that acted as the repository of a culture's collective wisdom. The storytellers of ancient communities were among the most revered and venerated of citizens. Stories of heroism, courage, love, hope, renewal, charity, and all other matters deemed important were told and retold in the verbal tradition of passing knowledge to the next generation. Stories today are just as important for transferring knowledge as they ever were. In fact, when significant cultural change occurs, it is often as a result of a powerful story, movie, or other metaphorical medium. Yet, as trainers, we may unconsciously neglect this potent means of learning.

Perhaps, we're not as practiced anymore in the verbal tradition of storytelling. Or maybe we don't know how to find or incorporate meaningful stories. The truth, however, is that good stories are everywhere. Our own lives are full of potential parables; all we have to do is see with the eyes of a storyteller. Stories encompass a whole realm of metaphorical expression. You might choose to use a simple joke, a personal experience, a news article, a current event, a folktale, a fairytale, a song, or a metaphor. All of these story devices can teach us something about the world in which we live, while triggering our emotions, tapping into our unconscious, and stimulating visual images that foster recall. Now let's take a look at the principles that hold the bricks of the TrainSmart model together.

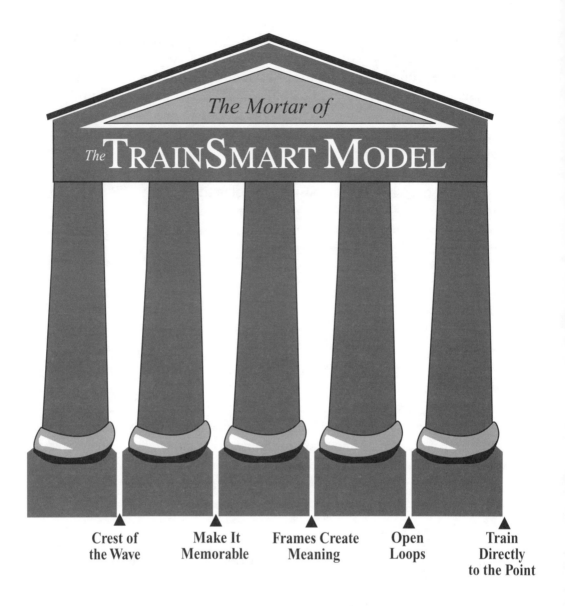

The Mortar of

The TRAINSMART MODEL

| Crest of the Wave | Make It Memorable | Frames Create Meaning | Open Loops | Train Directly to the Point |

1. Crest of the Wave

Way out in the distance, a swell begins to build. It is slow and steady at first, gradually gaining height and momentum as it moves ever closer to shore. Arching to a crest, the wave reaches critical mass, peaks, and crashes down over itself. The water rolls forward and finally dissipates as it washes up on the sandy shore. This simple metaphor demonstrates the natural rhythm of the learning process in the training room.

Simply put, much like waves building, peaking, then crashing down, there are swells, crests, and tumbles in the training environment. When a learner's ability to draw useful information from a given mode of instruction has been maximized, the *crest of the wave has been reached*. At this point it is in the best interest of everyone to shift to some alternate manner of instruction or to engage in some distinct change of pace that will refocus interest and attention.

This means trainers must become skilled observers and listeners. What is the sound level in the room? Are participants on or off task? Are they sitting on the edge of their seats or rocking back and forth in them? What is the energy level? Is it time for a change of pace? Do learners need to move around or take a break? These are the questions trainers must ask themselves moment by moment. If they ignore these vital cues, participants may grow increasingly uncomfortable, hesitant, and resistant. Eventually trainers could end up with a "difficult" group, unaware that their own timing, or lack of it, stimulated the dynamic to begin with.

The most effective trainers are responsive to the waves of interest generated in the room; they notice them and make the appropriate adjustments. Yet training is a living art. Your effectiveness is completely dependent upon your ability to stay present in the moment and respond to the energy and reactions of the participants. Even when the many environmental factors that impact a training are perfect—the room temperature, furniture arrangement, and type of equipment, the question still remains...

How long can participants effectively pay attention?

While answers will always vary among individuals and situations, academic studies suggest that, on average, adults can only fully pay attention in a new learning situation for about 15 minutes at a time. Yes, this figure is correct: 15 minutes, at most. And, in addition, learners tend to forget information presented in the middle of a session, so we need to maximize the beginnings and ends of a learning segment. So what does this means to you? In the training environment, we need to divide and conquer. Where traditionally, a short break may have been included in the middle of a 1-hour lecture, the crest principle proposes a more dynamic and flexible schedule that allows for frequent learning shifts and breaks. Rather than one long learning session, think of your training plan like a menu with hors-d'oeuvres, a main course, and dessert. Between meals provide brain breaks and movement activities. Beware of information overload: When the wave crests, it's time to change the pace.

Few trainers lament that they have too much time for instruction. You won't often hear them say things like, "Gosh, what am I going to do with all this free time?" It just doesn't happen. In fact, it is often the opposite, with frustration setting in over not having sufficient time to cover the material in an effective manner. Given this reality, trainers commonly continue to speak past the point that participants are able to effectively absorb new content.

 Instead, we need to allow participants the time to process new information through a variety of modalities (talking, reading, editing notes, brainstorming, or watching a video). This sets up a double win situation: On one hand, participants have the time to reorganize their thoughts, make connections, and consolidate information for long-term memory, while trainers are able to better assess the progress of the training and take a break themselves. Consequently, everyone comes back refreshed and refocused. This is what training smarter is all about.

If you're not riding the crest of the wave, chances are, you may find yourself beneath it.

2. Frames Create Meaning

Consider this scenario: A trainer introduces an exercise with only one brief remark, "Welcome to The Maze! Here's how the game is played." He then explains how to play the game, but learners are skeptical and hesitant about participating. Why might this happen?

On closer inspection, it is apparent that the trainer did not effectively *frame* the activity. Learners are busy wondering, why should we do this? What's the point? How does this relate to me, the topic, or my work? Without a frame, the participants understandably decide the activity is irrelevant and turn their attention elsewhere. Given the manner in which participants respond to the activity, the trainer decides to try a different approach.

The next day, he introduces the activity to a new group as follows: "Welcome to The Maze! The Maze is a puzzle. While solving it, several issues may emerge that will foster our understanding of innovation and creativity. When everyone experiences the simulation firsthand, it multiplies the richness and relevancy of our discussion that will follow the exercise."

With this frame, participants are able to grasp the learning purpose and significance of the exercise. They prepare themselves for the activity and the discussion to follow. The frame has successfully provided meaning.

3. Make It Memorable

The skilled trainer presents material in a manner that assists participants in remembering it easily and naturally. When trainers disregard this critical aspect of instruction, long-term retention of the material is significantly reduced. Our own familiarity with the material gives us the edge in creating a memory strategy suitable for the material; whereas, the primary job of the learner is to first comprehend the new material. How memorable are your presentations? What strategies can you use to make them even more memorable? Memory strategies are addressed throughout *TrainSmart*; here's a preview of some.

The value of storytelling and engaging emotions has already been addressed, but these two strategies can't be overemphasized. In addition, you can help learners remember important concepts with mnemonic strategies, such as acrostics and acronyms. The acronym HOMES, for example, has helped many U.S. children learn the names of America's five Great Lakes: Huron, Ontario, Michigan, Erie, and Superior. Also, applying the sound of a new word to a more familiar word assists learners in remembering unfamiliar vocabulary, and songs are a wonderful way to cue the subconscious mind. Almost every American youngster, for example, learned (and still learns) the alphabet to the tune of "Twinkle, Twinkle, Little Star." Mnemonic techniques, while primarily used today by younger learners, can be utilized by people of all ages. Everyone remembers more when we provide the brain with additional connections and cues.

Another memory strategy you'll discover in *TrainSmart* is *involving* participants in the learning, rather than *telling* them about it. You've probably heard this axiom: If you really want to know something, teach it. Asking participants to teach or lead aspects of the training is a highly effective technique for enhancing recall. Asking participants to share their level of prior learning or experience with the subject at hand early in the training also engages and stimulates recall by building on prior knowledge. Even simple partner exchanges can positively impact participants' long-term memory. A training environment accompanied by laughter, joy, and celebration is the ultimate memory builder. And lastly, help participants remember by limiting your presentation and material to that which is digestible in the allotted time period. Before any training plan is finalized, be certain to consider just how memorable you've made it.

4. Open Loops

It was the first morning of a 2-day technical training seminar. Participants were learning to repair a new walkie-talkie that would soon be sold in stores. As the session began, the trainer passed out a walkie-talkie to each person. When all the participants had received one, she asked that they turn them on. None of the units worked. She then said,

"Each device has some sort of problem: I personally saw to that. Now, here's a $20.00 bill. If you can fix your walkie-talkie, or anyone's around you in the next 5 minutes, the money is yours. Your 5-minute countdown begins now."

The trainees launched into the repair process—taking their walkie-talkies apart, interacting with others around them, and problem solving. When the 5-minute time period was up, none of the units had been repaired. "OK," said the trainer, "now let's learn how to make some money fixing these things." All eyes were on her, and it was clear that she had successfully employed the powerful training strategy known as an *open loop*.

By definition, an open loop is any statement, action, visual device, or other event that gives participants foreknowledge of what is coming. Open loops are used by trainers to set the stage for what is about to happen, to elicit curiosity, and to build suspense. There are many ways to achieve this effect.

You can do it with visuals, such as signs or posters placed around the room, or with a message displayed on the board or screen. A guitar placed in plain view, but not mentioned, can serve as an open loop if it is used later. Or perhaps you leave a box in plain view with a variety of colorful supplies poking out. Any event that arouses anticipation can be viewed as an open loop.

Ultimately, open loops create a dynamic that participants find irresistible: They need to "close the loop." Consider this metaphor: Have you ever been in a car, listening to one of your favorite songs when just before it ends, the DJ fades it out or begins speaking over the ending? Feeling cheated and irritated might be a very natural response to this situation. The longer you listened to the song, the stronger the loop became, and the more dissatisfaction you experienced when it was cut short. Once a loop has been opened, it is human nature to actively seek to close it.

Open loops are certainly an integral component of many books at the top of the New York Times best-selling fiction list. Avid mystery readers may remember the books of their youth, featuring Nancy Drew, Tom Swift, or the Hardy Boys. The authors of these classics frequently ended chapters with the hero or heroine in great peril, prompting the readers to race onto the next chapter. Today's best-selling authors, such as Stephen King, Danielle Steel, Tom Clancy, and Dean R. Koontz, while much more elegant in their delivery, utilize the same concept, although on a much more sophisticated level. One large loop contains the plot of the book, while it subsumes numerous smaller loops that are opened and closed as the story progresses.

Open loops also play a critical role in marketing and advertising. A well known jingle can get the consumer thinking about a certain restaurant or food. Colorful advertisements for exotic destinations can create the desire to travel; the only way to close the loop is to book a vacation. And some ad campaigns focus on making people feel like they are missing something if they don't possess a certain car, a new home, or the latest gadget.

Recognizing the universal appeal of open loops may help trainers realize the incredible potential of this tool in the training room. And while open loops come in many shapes and colors, their common denominator is they alert us to what is coming and its potential value. Given this perspective, participants are now more focused to receive the new information and remember it. The use of loops can be an effective component of any learning strategy, but they are never the entire strategy. Most importantly, remember that when a loop is opened, you've got to eventually close it!

5. Train Directly to the Point

A *little* knowledge, as the saying goes, can be a dangerous thing. In the training setting, however, *a lot* of knowledge can be an *even more* dangerous thing. Why? Because we forget one of the basic rules of effective instruction: *Train directly to the point!* Extraneous information should be limited to that which supports a deeper understanding of the topic. The following example illustrates this important principle:

The class was billed as an introduction to the company's email system. It was geared towards staff members who had little or no experience working with email. The trainer was a young man who had been working with computers most of his life. As participants filed in, he guided each of them to a computer station.

"I'd like to start by saying that using this system is really easy. You'll get the hang of it in no time at all, and pretty soon you'll be able to move on to some of the more interesting applications, such as creating a phone list, using an alias, and building databases. Why, you can even ...."

At this point he had already lost most of his participants. Although he spoke with enthusiasm, they were intimidated and unfamiliar with the trainer's language. They eventually filed out of the room feeling more intimidated of computers than they were prior to the session.

The next time the training was conducted, the trainer was better prepared. He had learned the principle of *training directly to the point*. The first thing he said was: "Welcome. Thank you for coming. Please turn on the computer that is sitting in front of you. Here's how that's done...."

At this point he waited patiently while participants searched for the appropriate button. It took a little time, but finally, everyone knew how to boot up the computer. At this point he asked them to turn it off again. Although they looked a bit puzzled, everyone complied. When all of the computers were off, the trainer asked everyone to step into the hallway where he began giving his next set of instructions. "When I open the door, please enter the room, go to any computer, and turn it on. Further instructions will be given once everyone has completed this step."

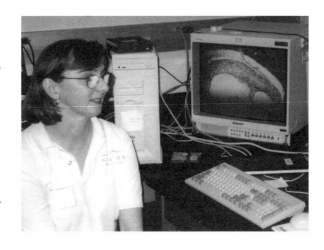

When all of the computers were up and running, the participants were congratulated. Most of them felt a bit silly about being acknowledged for accomplishing such a simple step, but deep down it was a confidence booster because it was so easy. The rest of the session proceeded in a similar sequential fashion—step by step, slow and purposeful, with each step repeated numerous times in sequence. By the time the training ended, each participant had demonstrated their ability to turn the computer on and off, to open the email program and their account, to send a message to someone else in the room, to read messages they had received, and to delete them. They demonstrated this to themselves not once, but many times over. The basic objectives of the course were accomplished with 100 percent participant success!

What was the basic difference between the original and revised approaches? The key difference was an understanding of the particular needs and experience levels of the participants, with the instruction geared accordingly. The bottom line? Avoid the temptation to add unnecessary information: Train directly to the point.

A Sample TrainSmart Schedule

✱ **Arrival:** Have upbeat music playing as participants enter the training area and get themselves situated.

✱ **Welcome and Greet:** Create involvement through various activities in which participants meet each other.

✱ **Content Introduction:** Introduce the colorful posters on the walls and have participants take a quick trip around the room to review them. The posters should reflect the key concepts of the training.

✱ **Opening Parable:** Tell a story that sets the scene or mood for the day. For example, you might share "The Traveler" (see parables in Part 3) to symbolize the importance of being open to new ideas and not rushing to judgement.

✱ **Distribution of Resources:** Before the training begins, hide the workbooks somewhere in the room. Now, have participants "gather their first gem" by standing up and finding a workbook. This activity doubles as a state-changer and a way to get the blood moving a little bit.

✱ **Plant an Open Loop:** Mention to participants that they might surprise themselves before the day is done. Hint that something intriguing will happen after lunch.

✱ **First Exploration:** Introduce/frame the activity before you begin.

✱ **Debriefing:** Ask the participants to write down at least three emotions they experienced while engaged in the exploration activity. Afterwards, ask for volunteers to share their ideas. Record these ideas on a flip chart.

-Morning Break-

Morning Session (Part 2)

- **Engager:** Bring participants back and refocus their attention with a brief 2-minute energizer.
- **Second Exploration:** Introduce/frame the activity.
- **Application:** Have participants pair up and consider how they might apply the learning to their work or home lives. Subsequent to the pair share, regroup and ask participants to share their responses while you once again record them on a flip chart page.
- **Make It Memorable:** Give participants the last 5 minutes of the morning to make notes about the most important concepts they've learned and how they might apply them personally and professionally.

-Lunch Break-

Afternoon Session (Part 1)

- **Engager:** Engage learners physically with a brief activity that is mildly active and encourages social interaction.
- **Close Open Loop:** Remind participants about the intriguing after-lunch activity, and then tell them they, themselves, will be teaching the rest of the session.
- **Exploration:** Have participants meet in small groups. Provide each group with an index card describing a pertinent concept learned in the morning session and with instructions for planning a 5-minute lesson based on that concept. Allow a set period of time in which to plan and practice the lesson they will be presenting to the rest of the group.

-Afternoon Break-

✖ **Final Energizer:** Have learners create and post "mind maps" related to the material they've been learning.

✖ **Application:** Have the groups present their 5-minute lessons.

✖ **Debriefing:** After the presentations, ask the class to provide feedback about what they felt worked and what didn't. This is also the time when the various pieces of the training are pulled together for a final recap.

✖ **Review:** Have participants stand up and review all of the posters on the walls. Provide an index card for them to record any final questions that they have. This is also a good time for participants to answer each other's questions as they walk around and discuss the posters and mind maps.

✖ **Ownership:** Ask everyone to complete a session evaluation that focuses on what they felt they received the most value from and that elicits ideas for how the course could be made even better in the future.

✖ **Closing Parable:** End with a story that reinforces your underlying theme. For example, you might tell the "Animal School" (see parables in Part 3) to reinforce the importance of training to an individual's strengths as opposed to forcing a square peg into a round hole. We all have natural gifts, we just need to recognize and strengthen them.

✖ **Closing Remarks:** Play some upbeat, inspiring music as you thank and acknowledge participants for their energy, enthusiasm, and attention.

This hypothetical training schedule demonstrates how the TrainSmart model looks in practice. Certainly, there are thousands of ways to translate the principles and/or modify them. The bottom line? ***Engage, Frame, Explore, Debrief, and Reflect!***

Part Two

25 Key Concepts
for Training Smarter

Part Two Preview

❧

The 25 Key Concepts

1. Acknowledgment
2. Bridges and Zones
3. Comfort Levels
4. Task Completion
5. Contrast
6. Precise Directions
7. Resource Distribution
8. Teach It Standing
9. Participant Inquiry
10. Adequate Response Time
11. Specify Response Mode
12. Patterning Interactions
13. Managing Distributions
14. Creative Note Taking
15. Target Language
16. Involve, Don't Tell
17. Ownership
18. Pause for Visuals
19. Press and Release
20. Purposeful Body Language
21. Visual Field Variations
22. Vocal Italics
23. Music Matters
24. Guiding Attention
25. Verbal Specificity

❧

Key Concept 1

ACKNOWLEDGMENT

 What It Is

Acknowledgment is a specific form of feedback and a powerful technique for helping learners succeed. Think about it; when your own efforts are positively acknowledged or affirmed by others, doesn't your motivation soar? At the very least, it makes you feel good. "Feeling good" is an influence we often underestimate and underutilize in the learning environment. When we acknowledge people, they feel recognized and affirmed.

 Why It's Important

Trainers who consistently acknowledge the efforts of participants, regardless of the results of those efforts, provide an important kind of encouragement, one that is essential to the learning process. Consider the image of a sail boat out on the open water. Imagine what happens to it as it encounters heavy winds on the open sea. In such conditions, its efforts are undoubtedly hampered. In a training room, the

same idea applies. If participants are acknowledged, but inconsistently, or worse, ignored or reprimanded for their best efforts, the "ship of learning" can be thrown off course, perhaps never to recover. Keep your participants moving forward, even in the face of strong resistance or challenging circumstances. When the ship of participant learning encounters a steady breeze to fill its sails, the vessel moves forward with a minimum of effort on the trainer's part. This represents the ideal learning and training environment. The best way to create this atmosphere is to provide consistent reinforcement using multiple types of acknowledgment.

 # How to Incorporate It

Trainers who consistently rely on multiple forms of encouragement elicit higher response levels from participants. To be effective, the encouragement must be genuine, focused on the specific efforts of an individual, and provided frequently enough to keep learners on course. In the training environment trainer-to-participant acknowledgment is the most common form. Perhaps a trainer responds to a solicited answer with something like, "That's correct" or "Good." Or maybe the trainer says, "Thank you" when participants complete an assignment on time. Or, we see a trainer give an occasional pat on the shoulder. But what's missing here?

A consistent theme runs through all of these situations: In each of them, it is the trainer providing the acknowledgment. This trainer-to-participant flow of reward and praise, although useful at times, does not provide sufficient acknowledgment in most learning situations—especially when the ratio of learners to trainer is high. When we don't move beyond this trainer-centered model of acknowledgment, we deprive learners of other positive feedback opportunities that can also support learning.

Why not spread the responsibility for acknowledgment around to include the participants? In the process, you will double the involvement of learners and lessen your own load. And ultimately, you will have created a more dynamic training environment. Consider the following acknowledgment possibilities when designing your next training program:

Self-Acknowledgment
Have participants assess their own learning by completing a questionnaire or survey on a recent topic of learning. If it is identified as a "quiz" or "test" in any way, its power as an acknowledgment tool may be minimized.

Rather, emphasize that it is a feedback mechanism for learners to assess their own strengths and weaknesses and to increase their understanding.

Peer Acknowledgment

In interactive learning environments, participants will work together in various ways. After group interactions, encourage participants to acknowledge others for their contributions to the team. Compliments between participants go a long way towards building learner confidence. After completing an activity, you can encourage learners, for example, to review each other's work and identify the positive aspects of it.

Physical Acknowledgment

Athletes use a wide variety of actions to congratulate each other for their successes, some of which work well in the training room. The practice of giving each other high-five's, for example, is a powerful means for acknowledging others' efforts. This simple technique is especially effective when the group has been engaged in a physical activity.

These suggestions are merely a sampling of what's possible. Trainers are encouraged to continue seeking other means of participant-to-participant acknowledgment, feedback, and appreciation. There are many!

 # When to Use It

It is useful to consider what actions might trigger acknowledgment in the training environment. Should it only occur when participants do something correct or something the presenter likes, appreciates, or values? While acknowledgment in these cases may be valid, if we stop here, we're missing a whole realm of possibilities for extending this critical concept.

What happens when acknowledgment is given even for small successes or honest endeavors that nevertheless fall short of mastery? This is perhaps the most important time to provide acknowledgment. Regardless of results, *honest effort* itself is commendable and the only reliable way to gain mastery of anything. When people see that their efforts will be rewarded with appreciative words and actions, they are generally prompted to try again, perhaps even harder. Participants who receive steady encouragement and positive feedback for their efforts are more inclined to stay mentally, physically, and emotionally involved—an essential condition for achieving mastery.

When *Not* to Use It

While it's important to *consistently* acknowledge the efforts of learners throughout a training, doing so to excess can reduce the impact of this technique. If trainers provide *constant* praise, learners may perceive it as contrived or disingenuous. They may even become distracted and annoyed, which could lead to a breakdown in learning. However, don't miss the opportunity to provide acknowledgment when participants have exerted effort towards a specific task or learning activity, regardless of the result.

 ## A Real-Life Training Example

The setting is a weeklong training for people who have been with the organization for at least 5 years and are looking to move into management. As the training winds down, a questionnaire is distributed to the participants. The final question is rather unique and baffling. It asks, "What's the name of the head custodian responsible for the building that houses our organization?"

Most of the participants are stumped. Since the question appears to be random, most of them decide it must be a joke and leave the question unanswered. When everyone has completed the assessment, someone asks the trainer if the final question was important. He replies,

> "Definitely! Success comes not just from *what* you know,
> it also depends on *who* you know. In your lifetime you will
> meet many people. Each of them is significant and deserves
> your attention, even if all you do is smile and say hello."

When participants come to value acknowledgment as a critical part of the learning environment, they also begin to realize its value in the larger context. Ultimately, they'll begin to offer it more frequently. Is there really a more basic and critical lesson for future managers than understanding the importance of honest, purposeful acknowledgment of others' efforts? Hey, well done...you've just completed key concept one!

Key Concept 2

BRIDGES AND ZONES

 What It Is

The use of *Bridges and Zones* represents a training technique for guiding participants' moods, internal responses, and states of learning readiness. Various *zones* or physical locations in the learning environment can be used by trainers, much like actors use areas on a stage, to stimulate participants' unconscious expect-
ations and to create transitions or *bridges* between different modes of learning. Bridges can be built, for example, through intentional alterations in tone of voice and gesture as trainers move between zones. Bridges and zones provide learners with cognitive and emotional connections that facilitate the learning process.

There are at least three distinct zones of instruction that trainers can use to prepare participants for prospective modes of learning:

1. The first zone is the area nearest the chalkboard, easel, or white board—the space furthest from the audience. This is the *instructional zone*, where content is delivered and visuals are usually located. When you move to this location, participants know that new information is about to be presented and that it's time to focus their attention, organize materials, and prepare to take notes. To build the bridge between this zone and your learners, modulate your voice evenly for content delivery and use gestures that clarify and support the explanation.

2. The second zone is closer to the audience—a few feet from the chalk board to a few feet in front of the podium. This is called the *facilitation zone*, an area useful for facilitating casual interaction with and among participants. You can use this zone to respond to participants' questions or when soliciting answers from them. When you shift to this area, the audience immediately knows that a different level of interaction is expected, and they can adjust their thinking accordingly. Create a connection with your learners while in this zone by making your tone of voice more casual and conversational and using inviting gestures.

3. The third zone is the area closest to the audience (or even among them) and is called the *directional zone*. The close proximity to the participants, as you move among them, intensifies the impact of the information being given and is, therefore, useful for giving directions or mobilizing participants. Use a clear and commanding voice with gestures that are large enough to encompass the entire room.

 ## Why It's Important

Trainers can use the technique of bridges and zones to set the stage for learning, create a constructive and focused climate, trigger positive emotions, provide smooth transitions from one task to another, and engage more participants. Just as children need regular schedules and rituals to depend on, adult  learners find comfort in them, as well. A moderately predictable environment provides a sense of security, thus, freeing up the brain for learning. And, just as learners need rituals to transition smoothly from one topic to the next, predictable cues for transitioning to another mode of learning is helpful as well. Bridges and zones represent an effective tool for facilitating these transitions.

How to Incorporate It

Consider the following suggestions for effectively using bridges and zones in your next workshop:

✖ If you wish to facilitate a sense of relaxation and emotional safety at the start of your training, consider using the *facilitation zone* to initiate casual conversation and interaction between you and your participants. Maintain a relaxed posture and informal tone of voice.

✖ Establish your zones early in the workshop and be consistent in the way you use them. Don't wait, for example, until the workshop is half over to start making use of the facilitation zone. Use each at least three times, so that a familiarity is established with the areas and their respective learning modes.

✖ Make the transition from one zone to the other smooth and casual, rather than abrupt or overt. Practice switching from one zone and its mode of learning to another prior to the training.

 # When to Use It

While frequent shifts between zones are recommended, there are a few circumstances when using this strategy is especially important, such as (1) at the beginning of a session when establishing rapport, (2) when a change in learning mode occurs, (3) at the close of a session, (4) when providing important instructions, (5) when making a critical point, and (6) when soliciting audience participation. Clear, deliberate, and consistent use of your bridges and zones throughout the course of a training can make a world of difference in the readiness of learners.

 # When *Not* to Use It

As you increase your awareness and utilization of the bridges and zones concept, you'll see that the key is to avoid using the strategy inconsistently. When trainers wander around the room unconsciously between zones, for example, they give the learner permission to wander (mentally), as well.

The more purposeful the trainer is in his or her delivery, the more focused participants are in their acquisition of the information. To be effective, use bridges and zones in a well-planned, consistent, and purposeful way.

 # A Real-Life Training Example

It's the start of a 2-day corporate workshop in which teamwork is the primary focus. All the participants have arrived and the trainer is ready to begin. She signals the group by casually approaching an unoccupied desk near the front row. Sitting comfortably on the edge of the desk, she says,

> "Good morning. Welcome to today's workshop. I'd like to begin by providing an opportunity for us to get acquainted with one another. As we go around the room, let's introduce ourselves to the group and share why we're here. Feel free to share any experiences, good or bad, in which teamwork played an important role in your personal or professional life."

The participants and the trainer spend a few minutes introducing themselves and sharing their thoughts and experiences. The trainer thanks the group and heads back toward the whiteboard. As she points to some text written on the whiteboard, she says,

> "Now let's focus on the five key principles of effective team work. These principles will form the framework for everything we learn today, so you may want to takes notes."

The trainer is effectively leading the group's focus as she uses bridges and moves between zones to make a smooth transition from one learning mode to the next. Learners unconsciously follow her lead, becoming more and more comfortable as the trainer demonstrates an expert command of the audience and learning environment. She has successfully established an initial level of connection between the zone she is using and the mode of instruction within that zone.

Key Concept 3

COMFORT LEVELS

 What It Is

The concept of *Comfort Levels* refers to the benefits of paying careful attention to the physical and emotional concerns of learners during activities that require them to interact with one another. This is a tall order when we consider that interpersonal skills, social and cultural norms, and comfort levels can greatly vary among individuals. The most effective trainers, however, have learned to incorporate a host of techniques to help people generally feel safe in the learning environment despite these differences.

 Why It's Important

The risk inherent in facilitating interactive exercises is that they can potentially create physical and psychological discomfort among participants, which, if not handled with the utmost respect and sensitivity, can lead to a breakdown in learning. While this concept may seem obvious, it should not be taken lightly. A rapid and serious decrease in enthusiasm and cooperation usually occurs when students are even slightly uncomfortable

and, in extreme cases, may lead to outright rebellion. However, when trainers are able to create a sense of physical relaxation and emotional ease among participants, a bond of trust can quickly develop between trainer and students and among students themselves, allowing the boundaries of learning to be stretched.

How to Incorporate It

Some of the techniques veteran trainers use to establish a sense of safety in the learning environment include the following:

- Always give participants the permission to "pass" if they wish on any aspect of an exercise or activity.

- Always establish ground rules before starting an exercise (i.e., when it's appropriate to ask questions or give feedback, time expectations, transition instructions, etc.)

- If the setting is not appropriate for the expression of strong emotions, do not facilitate an activity that may stimulate them.

- Provide an initial road map of the exercise before starting, so learners know what to expect.

- Be sensitive to how groups are organized/selected. Everyone should always feel included.

- If a group activity requires a leader or other facilitation roles, organize your method for establishing them prior to the activity and with sensitivity to involving everyone.

- Establish trust incrementally between trainer and participants before plunging into potentially emotional situations. Start with gentle, nonthreatening activities and progress as trust is established.

- Preface activities that might potentially bring up strong emotions with an acknowledgment that it is "okay" to move through them in what ever way emerges. Have tissues readily available for exercises that might elicit tears.

- ✖ Always plan a debriefing time at the conclusion of an exercise. This allows participants to deal with any unresolved questions or concerns and puts some closure on the experience.

- ✖ Many people feel uncomfortable closing their eyes in large group settings. Minimize activities that require learners to do this until trust has been established, and limit the time to approximately 10 seconds initially. Always provide the option of doing the activity without eyes closed.

- ✖ When an activity requires people to cross over the normal boundaries of their personal space, be sensitive to the distress that this can cause some individuals. Watch participants carefully for signs of stress. Adjust the physical parameters of the exercise if necessary.

- ✖ When an activity requires unfamiliar participants to sit in pairs facing each other, the arrangement can quickly turn awkward. Watch for signs of discomfort or idle conversation and provide participants with a reason to turn away from each other in such instances. Give pairs instructions about what to do once they've completed the task (i.e., to move on to the next one, take a break, sit down, etc.).

- ✖ How long can we expect participants to remain fully focused on new material being presented to them? Although this varies between individuals, a good rule is to facilitate participant dialogue every 15 to 20 minutes.The best trainers create frequent purposeful opportunities for dialogue throughout a learning session, while varying them in structure and function (i.e., small groups, dyads, the large group, introduction time, breaking-the-ice activities, question-and-answer time, closure time, etc.).

✖ Do not put learners on the spot unless there is a clear, productive reason for doing so. Learners who feel embarrassed or threatened in any way will not have the focus necessary to listen and learn in a purposeful way. Always acknowledge or apologize to a participant in private should an unexpected, embarrassing, or uncomfortable situation occur. Let participants know you care about their feelings.

 ## When to Use It

While steps should be taken at every juncture to ensure the physical and psychological comfort of participants, perhaps the most important time to use this concept is during group activities, especially physical ones that require touching and close contact. The potential for perceived threat is intensified for many learners during such exercises, often stemming from a fear of looking foolish among one's peers or from past experience in similar situations.

 ## When *Not* to Use It

This concept should be in the forefront of every trainer's mind at all times. However, there may be an occasion in which (depending on the nature of the training), you purposefully want learners to experience the tension and bodily sensations of "fear" or "anxiety." Even in such rare cases as this, precautions must be taken so that learners know they have a choice and the freedom to not participate. Thus, even in these situations, the groundwork for "comfort" and safety must be laid. A foundation of trust, in such cases, is essential.

A Real-Life Training Example

In a workshop on teamwork, the trainer was leading an exercise commonly known as The Human Knot, in which clusters of participants joined hands randomly, creating a tangled knot of arms. The task was to figure out how to untangle the knot while staying connected to each other. After asking the groups to join hands, the trainer announced the following:

> "I bet you're all wondering what you're about to do! Well, actually, this activity is called The Human Knot! But before we begin, let me tell you a little bit about its background...."

The trainer then launched into a 3-minute history of the activity. What's wrong with this picture?

The problem, although probably obvious to you, was not so obvious to this trainer. Introducing the exercise while participants were left standing in awkward positions, holding sweaty hands with someone they didn't know, and while crossing general boundaries of personal space was not a decision that enhanced participants' sense of emotional safety and comfort. It wasn't long, in fact, before the participants released each other's hands and the exercise lost momentum. Worse yet, the participants, now slightly embarrassed or impatient, were going to be less inclined to trust the trainer's facilitation in future activities.

Key Concept 4

TASK COMPLETION

 **What It Is**

Effective trainers facilitate a sense of closure or *Task Completion* before moving from one topic to the next. The brain needs a little time to prepare for such a transition, and trainers can provide this by paying careful attention to the progression or steps in their lesson planning. Just as you might give a youngster, for example, a warning that the TV goes off in 5 minutes, we need to be conscious of preparing adult learners for the next step or expectation in the learning schedule before arriving there. We also need to deal with any lingering issues, questions, or concerns from the previous activity that might otherwise distract individuals and divide their attention.

Why It's Important

Most of us have experienced a training or seminar that felt disjointed, awkward, or even frustrating, without being able to put a finger on why. In contrast, when a lesson is well planned and includes task completion and smooth transitions, learners glide through the process without too much emotional interference. It is important, therefore, that as trainers we stay aware of the flow of the session from one stage to the next. For example, when presenting an exercise or activity to a group, always explain what your time expectations are, what learners should do when they're finished, and what the following agenda item will be. Afterwards, debrief the group and answer any remaining questions or concerns. This process reinforces important conclusions and provides closure while also developing interest in the next step in the learning process.

How to Incorporate It

One technique that works well to is write down in one or two succinct sentences the primary goal(s) of the exercise or activity. Then make sure these are among your final words when you close the learning session. Since our attention bias is strongest at both the beginning and the end of a session, it's a good idea to take advantage of learners' expanded memory capacity during these windows of time. Whether completing a single topic, task, or an entire training session, keep the following key elements in mind:

- Focus learners' attention on a sense of *accomplishment*. Affirm, for example, that some *forward movement* in the learning process took place. Participants more readily leave a learning segment behind to transition to the next if they feel they've learned something new and useful. If this sense of cognitive gain is not perceived, participants will be less likely to "follow" as you lead them through the next learning task. Instead, they're contemplating the possibility that their return on their investment is not adequate—a mental state that clearly won't facilitate receptivity and concentration. Some closing questions to encourage learners to consider are (1) How does what I just learned apply to me or the circumstances in my life, now or in the future? (2) How much of the lesson (in percentage terms or on a scale of 1-to-10) did I follow and understand? (3) Where might there be holes in my understanding? (4) How might this new skill/information benefit me personally/professionally? And, (5) What memory tool might help me remember what I've learned today?

- For new learning to be remembered, it must be *internalized*—a concept also known as a "self-convincing" state. Thus, students not only need to understand the concept in principle, they also need to know how it applies specifically to them. They must also believe it. Closing rituals, therefore, are most effective when they help the learner *embody* new concepts. For example, in small groups have learners share their introspections or self-discoveries about the topic or process. Some questions to facilitate this discussion might include (1) What did I learn? (2) How does what I learned impact others and me? And, (3) How do I feel about what I've learned? This type of closing exercise can also be helpful for eliciting feedback to improve your future training sessions.

* *Closures* and task completions can range from a simple, one-sentence instruction to a complex set of activities and rituals. But completion is so crucial to meaningful learning that it's worth setting aside at least 10 percent of your entire presentation for this purpose. Even if you're rushed or running out of time, don't omit this important part of learning. If your presentation is 10 minutes, your closure should be at least a few minutes. If you're doing a 50-minute presentation, conduct your closure in the last 5 to 8 minutes. A 1-day training might have a closure that is 20 to 30 minutes in length.

* When you invite participants to raise their hands, remember to tell them to put them down. While this instruction may seem unnecessary, it's amazing how often participants wait for it!

* When inviting participants to take a deep breath, be sure to instruct them to exhale as well. Again, this may seem like an unnecessary step, but many a training participant has been seen patiently holding their breath while waiting for a cue from the facilitator to exhale.

* When presenting a new activity, be certain participants are brought to a point of successful completion before moving on. Frustrated learners are often unable to pay attention to the next task, as they remain mentally stuck on the last topic. In some cases, they may simply give up completely on any subsequent learning.

* When closing a multiple-day session or when disbanding for a break, be sure to inform participants of what they can expect when they return. Unless there is a specific structural reason to *not* do so, prepare learners for what's ahead.

When to Use It

At the very least, a final closing exercise or activity ought to be initiated after almost every learning session—whether it is an hour-long, day-long, or multi-day-long training. In addition, closing rituals between learning segments can clear the air for the next topic. Perhaps the most important time to emphasize completion, however, is at the conclusion of an entire training—an important time to tie all the loose ends together and relate the parts to the whole. This simple act can dramatically reinforce recall.

When *Not* to Use It

There are occasions when a trainer might wish to purposefully leave an activity or exercise unclosed. For example, You might want learners to brainstorm ideas overnight or assimilate a concept on their own before drawing conclusions about it later. When used sparingly and purposefully this can be a good strategy for stimulating critical analysis. For the most part, however, learners won't tolerate lack of closure for very long.

Another point to keep in mind is that people work and think at different speeds. Therefore, always provide adequate time for most (if not all) participants to complete an activity. Plan time for questions and/or concerns to be addressed. While we can't always give every participant the time he or she might prefer to fully accomplish a task, we can be careful not to cram too many learning goals into a single session. Teaching too much information in a limited time frame rushes everyone through the learning process and bombards participants with more content than they can reasonably digest in the time allotted.

A Real-Life Training Example

Be careful not to leave learners hanging at any given stage of an exercise or activity. The following example reflects how an uncompleted action can leave some learners in an uncomfortable position and negatively impact the learning of the entire group:

At the front of the training room, a large piece of paper is taped to the wall stretching from floor to ceiling. Two participants are invited to come forward. Each is given a pen and asked to mark the highest point they can reach on the paper. The trainer than asks them to close their eyes and visualize themselves reaching higher. After a minute, the participants open their eyes and try again. Both are able to reach even higher the second time around. The group applauds the demonstration and the trainer spends the next several minutes discussing the power of positive thinking.

The trainer is passionate about his topic and provides examples, both current and historical, to support his beliefs about the power of visualization and positive thinking. However, despite his considerable enthusiasm, it becomes apparent that the audience's attention has wandered. Can you guess why?

What became of the two people who participated in the demonstration? Both of them were left standing at the front of the room. Since they had not been asked to return to their seats, they remained where they were, wondering whether they would be needed again. As the trainer continued his presentation, they became fidgety and restless. One eventually sat cross-legged on the floor. The audience's reaction finally alerted the trainer that he had forgotten to thank and excuse the volunteers. He paused for a moment and asked the class to give them a round of applause. At this point he continued speaking, although a considerable amount of time had been lost while everyone was distracted.

Key Concept 5

CONTRAST

 What It Is

Contrast, as defined for training purposes, refers to the human brain's tendency to identify certain elements that are different from others in the immediate environment. Black letters stand out against a white background. A large red ball is easily distinguishable in a field of green grass. One person standing still in a crowd of moving people is easy to single out. And, a car alarm sounding off in an otherwise quiet parking lot can be heard at considerable distance. This is a critical strategy for effective teaching and training in that it can be used to help focus and guide learners' attention.

Degrees of contrast vary depending on the level of differentiation between the elements. The differences can be based on color, movement, texture, auditory cues, or any variety of sorting variables. Trainers can use this principle of contrast to emphasize key concepts and reinforce recall.

Why It's Important

During the course of a learning session, participants are bombarded with masses of sensory data. Somehow the target information (or learning goals) must stand out in the learners' minds. Contrast is an effective method for spotlighting the central ideas. With repetition and contrast, comprehension and recall increases. As key concepts are encoded into long-term memory, a strong foundation is built to sustain the next stage of learning.

How to Incorporate It

Consider some of the following strategies for integrating contrast into your next training session:

✖ In addition to using contrast to highlight single key points *within* a training segment, use it to create a differentiated learning environment on a larger scale. For example, if a quiet, more focused portion of instruction is followed by a more active session, both become unique in comparison to each other.

✖ Suppose a brief lecture contains one central idea. Consider having all participants stand and listen for one minute to this impor- tant point. Then have them *remain* standing while they spend a moment briefly dis- cussing this point with people near them. This  change of physical posture will serve to differentiate the piece from the rest of the information. Another option is to have them stand and dis- cuss this idea with each other *after* the point has been introduced.

✖ Take the group outside or to another location at a key moment in the session. Once there, teach the primary idea, have learners briefly discuss it, then return to the training room. While the decision to phy- ically relocate the class may seem a somewhat dramatic choice, this drama is the very element that can help participants remember what they learned.

✖ Turn the lights down and set a reflective mood when you want partici- pants to relax. This provides contrast (therefore, a state change) for a closing activity or visualization exercise.

✖ Integrate color, music, humor, and movement to highlight critical information.

When to Use It

Contrast ought to be used whenever you want to emphasize a key point. Prior to the session, identify the most important information you want to convey and spotlight these learning goals throughout the training.

 # When *Not* to Use It

If overused, this technique loses some of its power. This is why it is so important to isolate in advance the most important information and create a plan for emphasizing it. Be sure to use contrast consistently—that is, purposefully spotlight *only* that information that you deem to be imperative.

 ## A Real-Life Training Example

During a session on workplace safety, the trainer found an effective way to maximize the impact of a key point with the use of movement. He presented the point initially in a fast-paced, exuberant way, using plenty of large gestures, a dramatic tone of voice, intense facial expressions, and physical comedy. Finally, when it was clear his point had been made, he stepped into the center of the room and stood completely still for several seconds. While pausing, he made eye contact with the participants, and with a minimum of movement, restated the original point. The contrast between the two styles of presenting, reflected in the trainer's tone of voice and physical gestures, as well as the pause before speaking, clearly had a dramatic impact. The audience was mesmerized, their attention focused, their recall solidified.

Key Concept 6

PRECISE DIRECTIONS

 **What It Is**

Precise Directions in a training context represents a critical element in the learning process. Top trainers not only provide clear, sequential, and succinct instructions, they mobilize and guide students with language that builds credibility and trust. Giving precise directions is truly an art form unto itself, and much like a work of art, it may be more difficult to create than one might initially think.

Each stage of a learning segment—the opening, frame, group activity, debriefing, and closure—requires a shift in communication and some directions. When trainers transition into direction-giving mode, sentence structure and rhythm, tone of voice, proximity to the audience, and body language shift.

 Why It's Important

Even in a conventional classroom, teachers need to give directions surprisingly often. In a highly interactive training, even more direction is necessary. Whether an activity requires only a brief explanation or a whole sequence of steps (outlined on the board or projection screen), realize that before participants can be expected to move smoothly and effectively through the learning activity, they need to clearly understand each step of the process and what's expected of them.

A lack of clarity in direction giving presents a variety of problems. Participants who are unclear about the process may hesitate to involve themselves for fear of doing something wrong. They may quickly wander off task, or worse, think they are on task when they're not. Few trainers enjoy the moment when a participant raises a hand in the middle of a process and utters the dreaded question, "What are we *supposed* to be doing?"

If you give unclear directions too many times (or even once), nothing less than your own credibility is at stake. It might not be long before learners start thinking, What else is he going to say that won't make sense? Who is this guy? Could he really be an expert? Obviously, no trainer wants these thoughts filtering through the minds of participants. The key is to realize before your training ever starts just how important it is to provide precise directions in all situations.

 ## How to Incorporate It

The delivery of directions should be *congruent* with the message. Does the trainer's tone of voice support the primary message? Are the trainer's gestures adding to the participants' clarity of understanding? Is the wording clear, succinct, and vivid? Is the trainer's proximity commanding participants' highest level of attention? Are the directions provided in a succinct manner with an edge that implies the process will be both enjoyable and productive? Each of these elements can add to or detract from the lesson depending on quality of delivery. Delivering precise directions is a unique mode of instruction that has a specific purpose—to mobilize learners into some sort of action. Here are some tips for incorporating both congruency and clarity into your directions:

✖ Be short, precise, and specific. Practice directions in advance to cut out any unnecessary words. For example, instead of saying, "I want you all to turn to page 42," simply say, "Please turn to page 42."

✖ Give instructions one at a time. Do not bombard students with multiple instructions without allowing ample time for task completion between them or without perhaps providing a written review of the steps involved.

✖ Wait until everyone's attention is focused before giving directions. If participants have just arrived, or are just finishing a task, or are looking at notes or textbooks, get their full attention first. If necessary, deal with any lingering issues, and then re-request the full attention of everyone before introducing the next task.

✖ Modulate your tone of voice and use body language that is *congruent* with the type of directions you are giving. For example, when asking participants to stand up, you might increase the pitch of your voice on the word "up" and raise your arms in an inviting gesture. When asking learners to close their eyes for an activity, you might want to lower your voice, turn down the lights, and perhaps even close your own eyes before speaking.

✖ Make eye contact with as many (if not all) of your participants as possible as you deliver the directions. Check with the group to ensure they understand the steps involved and the purpose of the activity before starting.

✖ As described in Key Concept 2, *Bridges and Zones*, make sure you move to the appropriate *directional zone* when delivering instructions. This is the area closest to the audience. Its proximity helps focus learners' attention and prepare them for action.

✖ Establish precise time frames when providing directions. For example, if a trainer says, "We'll be moving into groups shortly," participants may immediately begin mentally sorting themselves into groups and miss any subsequent information. They might start wondering how long is *shortly*? I better hurry; there's not much time to think! Whom do I want (or *not* want) in my group? And what are we going to have to do then? With all this internal interjection, learners' focus is divided (if not completely lost). A better approach is to say, "In 2 minutes, we'll be moving into preestablished groups." This is a much more precise direction.

When to Use It

For maximum impact, directions and explanations should be provided for each step of
the process. For example, when preparing
learners to take a quiz, instruct them about
what supplies they should have in front of
them, where to put their books and other
extraneous materials, and what the time
expectations are. When learners raise their
hands, also remind them to put them down.
If you ask a learner to write on the whiteboard or easel, instruct them also to sit down
when they're done. While providing verbal
instructions at every juncture may occasionally appear excessive, a lack of adequate
direction can lead to confusion, disruption,
divided attention, and impaired cognition.

 # When *Not* to Use It

In contrast, if a trainer gives directions constantly, repeatedly, or indis-
criminately, especially *during* activities that demand intense concentration,
participants can easily become distracted, disengaged, and frustrated. A
good example, and one that occurs all too often, is when trainers continue
to talk or repeat directions after students have begun concentrated work. At
this point, it is much better to answer individual questions in a quiet, one-
to-one manner.

A Real-Life Training Example

At one training, I was observing the proceedings from the back of the room when the trainer asked participants to read a specific line from their workbooks. She opened her own book to the appropriate page and said, "Please turn to page 12 and follow along with me." However, as she began to discuss the designated line in the book, I noticed that something wasn't right. While some of the participants had rapidly located the correct page and were following along, many had just found their workbooks, but had yet to find the correct page or line. The rest of the participants *were still looking for their workbooks.* They were busily looking under their chairs, checking their tables, or turning to see if they had left their workbooks at the back of the room. How much learning do you think was happening at this point? Not much.

A vital step in giving effective directions is to verify that each member of the audience is following along at the appropriate pace. Instead of continuing forward while leaving some members of the audience behind, this trainer could have paused and said, "If you have found page 12, please hold your hand in the air." At this point, she could have carefully looked over the group to verify that everyone was ready to continue.

Timing the delivery of directions and allowing sufficient pauses between each step in the sequence is essential. The best way to determine if your timing and pace is effective is to check in with your audience frequently and regularly while always taking the time to look and listen carefully. A trainer's gift of personal expression, built on a strong foundation of technical expertise and sensitivity to the needs of the participant, is an essential component to creating and delivering an effective learning session.

Key Concept 7

RESOURCE DISTRIBUTION

 ## What It Is

A consideration most trainers must contend with is how to cover all the necessary information in the allotted time. Thus, time efficiency is usually an important factor when preparing a lesson/training plan. The distribution of support materials is another time-related consideration. Although many presenters don't think twice about leaving participants in an idle holding pattern during *Resource Distribution*, the TrainSmart presenter elevates this

otherwise nonproductive downtime to a higher plane by providing a little humor, a state change, or a touch of novelty. Such unexpected elements can provide contrast, boost attention, increase motivation, and ultimately enhance cognition. In this context, the time spent distributing materials becomes purposeful and productive.

Why It's Important

When the distribution process takes more than 30 seconds, you run the risk of losing learners' attention to restlessness, sedation, or boredom. Therefore, do not leave participants idle while materials are passed out. Once a group's concentration has been lost, it may be difficult to reestablish. Also, since materials are often distributed at the *beginning* of a learning session, it is especially important to engage learners immediately and purposefully. This can be accomplished by requesting participants' help or, better yet, by elevating this otherwise mundane routine with a novel, funny, or energizing approach to the task.

 # How to Incorporate It

There are many inventive ways to distribute materials so that learners' attention is maintained throughout the process. The list below represents only a few of the many options available to the trainer:

* Distribute handouts (two alike to each learner) to half of the room. Then ask these learners to stand and deliver their extra handout to a learner on the opposite side. Give them a specific period of time (i.e., 30 seconds) to introduce themselves to each other before returning to their seats. Next time, reverse sides and have learners select someone new to introduce themselves to.

* If you plan to review and/or discuss a handout immediately after distributing it, organize the material in four to five separate stacks and locate them in various parts of the room. Divide participants into groups and have each group organize themselves around one of the stacks. Ask the members of each group to read the handout and discuss its content before reconvening for a large group discussion.

* Ask participants to move tables to the periphery and then to arrange the chairs in a circle in the center of the room. Pass out materials and ask for volunteers to read aloud before following up with a group discussion.

* Arrive early and place resource packets around the training room so that they are only slightly visible (i.e., under a table, behind a curtain, or beneath a ledge). When it's time to distribute them, announce that the course materials are hidden in strategic places around the room. Hold one up so participants know what they look like, and tell them that when you say "go," they'll have 1 minute to find a workbook for themselves and to make sure everyone around them has one, as well.

✖ Put on some high-energy music and ask participants to get up and take a handout from each of the stacks you have set up at the front of the room prior to the session. At the end of the "assembly line," have a stapler or binder available.

These strategies all have at least one thing in common: they get learners moving, interacting, and using their brains.

 # When to Use It

When participants are expected to be sedentary for too long they are apt to become tired. Thus, it is a good idea to incorporate strategic brief energy breaks throughout the training. A mental and physical state change is recommended approximately every 15 to 20 minutes. The distribution of materials can be an effective way to incorporate a productive state change. Integrate distribution needs with a stretch break, a surprise, or other energizing activity whenever time allows.

 # When *Not* to Use It

If you plan to distribute materials immediately following a fast-paced, energetic learning activity, consider taking a more conventional approach. Rather than energizing the group in this case, you'll want to give them time to catch their breath, relax a moment, and transition into the next learning segment.

A Real-Life Training Example

It was the first day of a training. Participants had arrived and taken their seats. The trainer had introduced herself, and was prepared to get the session underway. She picked up a stack of papers and faced the audience. Holding them up so everyone could see them, she said, "Here is the schedule for this training—the syllabus." She then approached the first row of participants and was about to pass them out when she paused. She announced, "Actually, if you're really interested in what's going to happen, it's up to you to get a syllabus!" With that, she threw the stack of papers high in the air, scattering them everywhere. The stunned participants stared at her for a moment, then quickly moved to pick up one of the papers strewn about.

Why did she behave in this bizarre way? Was it merely a random act of strangeness? Was she close to suffering a nervous breakdown? Or, was there a larger purpose behind her actions? In fact, when preparing for this course, this trainer had decided to let the participants know right from the start that not only were they going to have to take some responsibility for their own learning, the training would be unusual. She could have simply said that, but knew this surprise tactic would have more impact.

In this instance, the trainer realized that distributing the syllabus represented an opportunity to do something ordinary or a chance to do something *extra*ordinary. The participants were startled into being fully awake, and she could now build on the energy generated by this creative jump-start to her training.

Key Concept 8

TEACH IT STANDING

 ## What It Is

Teach It Standing is a technique that boosts cognition by getting participants out of their seats and onto their feet. Traditional *learning* environments have somehow become erroneously linked to *sitting*, when in fact, standing or stretching stimulates blood circulation, which enhances cognition. Conversely, sitting for extended periods of time has a sedating affect and can become physically uncomfortable—factors that impede concentration. In an interactive learning environment, there are plenty of opportunities to encourage standing rather than sitting. Teachers and trainers stand; why not learners?

 ## Why It's Important

Why do so many learners dread the training room? Perhaps because they're faced with sitting in a chair for most of the day. Certainly there is a time and place for sitting in the training environment, such as while taking a test or note taking, but trainers who expect learn-ers to sit for extended periods are likely to encounter a decrease in participants' attention, motivation, and recall.

How to Incorporate It

The following ideas reflect some simple strategies for integrating activities in which the participants stand:

✖ At the start of each training session, facilitate some deep breathing, stretching, and movement exercises to energize and prepare learners.

✖ Conduct a "getting-to-know-you" ritual in which participants stand and introduce themselves to two or three other participants.

✖ Ask participants to get up and form circles for small group interaction activities.

✖ Conduct a short demonstration in the front of the room and have learners gather around to watch.

✖ Break up 40- to 60-minute segments of seatwork with a brief energizer. For example, invite participants to get up and walk around the periphery of the room with a partner, discussing the content, while you play some fast, upbeat music.

✖ As discussed in the previous section, ask participants to gather supplies themselves instead of handing them out.

✖ Create opportunities for "carousel" activities. For example, have participants add their contributions or ideas to sheets of paper hanging on the walls around the training room.

✖ If possible, provide a space (usually at the back of the room) that is conducive for standing and moving about during the session. Clipboards can make it possible for participants to take notes while standing, as well.

✖ Conduct a closing activity that gets participants up and out of their chairs. For example, have the group gather in one large circle while offering and inviting individual acknowledgments.

When to Use It

Invite participants to stand, stretch their limbs, and energize their brains *anytime* during your training. In addition, facilitate a standing exercise, activity, or break approximately every 30 minutes.

 # When *Not* to Use It

 Of course there needs to be a balance between standing and sitting activities. Some learning activities, such as test taking, note taking, essay writing, and extensive reading, are obviously better suited for sitting. However, it is best to intersperse these tasks with standing breaks and activities. It is also important for participants to have the option to sit if they are unable to stand or don't want to participate in the activity. Try to limit standing activities to 3 to 5 minutes, as longer periods can be tiring for some and thus counterproductive to learning.

A Real-Life Training Example

It *seems* like a typical training setting. The participants come into the room and take a seat, prepared to remain there for the duration of the day. The trainer is at the front of the room arranging stacks of papers and workbooks, which the participants anticipate receiving shortly. Instead, as the remaining participants arrive and take their seats, the trainer introduces himself and asks the group to quickly move their chairs to the sides of the room. Bewildered, the participants comply, buzzing questions to one another about why they're doing this and what's coming next. The trainer then asks the participants to stand in a large circle in the center of the room, where each member is asked to introduce him or herself to the rest of the group. The trainer then thanks the participants and leads them through 5 minutes of deep breathing and stretching activities. As he concludes this energizing movement, he asks the group to return their chairs to their previous positions and to take a workbook and syllabus from the front of the room before returning to their seats.

In addition to providing an element of surprise, the trainer in this example was able to effectively energize and prepare his participants for a full day of learning. In addition, he created a sense of emotional safety by allowing participants to get to know one another at the start of the training. Thus, the trainer was able to accomplish two tasks at once—to stimulate and prepare the minds and bodies of his learners, and to foster a sense of camaraderie and group cohesiveness.

Key Concept 9

PARTICIPANT INQUIRY

 What It Is

Participant Inquiry is a technique whereby the trainer poses carefully worded questions to involve learners while minimizing emotional risk. Such questions encourage participants to reveal information about themselves and their experience with the subject matter in a way that does not leave them feeling "put on the spot." As learners are encouraged to share, they feel valued and acknowledged. If you do not know "who" is in your

audience, it may be presumptuous to assume you can effectively "train" them. Participant inquiry not only helps you determine the extent of your learners' knowledge and experience, it facilitates a sense of group cohesiveness as common ground is discovered and learners open up to each other.

 Why It's Important

The training environment (or, in fact, *any* new learning situation) can be scary for many individuals. If this sense of fear is not dispelled quickly and replaced with a sense of commonality among participants, learning can suffer. While scientists know that even a *minimal* level of threat can throw the brain into survival mode at the expense of concentration and higher-order thinking, they also know that a sense of group cohesion can facilitate an immediate sense of safety. What is considered threatening varies between individuals; however, when learners sense they will not be embarrassed or ridiculed before the group, and that they are valued and acknowledged for who they are and what they have to contribute, feelings of safety ensue. This leaves the brain free to focus on learning.

 # How to Incorporate It

Consider the following guidelines for incorporating participant inquiry:

✳ Preface group questions with words and phrases that elicit brief hand responses, yet still acknowledge individual experiences. Here are a few examples:

> Raise your hand if...?
> How many of you...?
> How many of you would like to...?
> How many of you have ever...?
> How many of you are going to one day...?
> How many of you believe that...?

✳ Prepare a series of questions to ask at the start of your training and at various points throughout. You'll want the questions to be relevant to the learning objectives, as well as to the participants themselves.

✳ Design safe questions that invite participants to talk about themselves, their experiences, where they're from, what they want out of the training, and why they're there. Questions that are *too* personal or not clearly related can embarrass participants and cause withdrawal—the opposite response from what you're seeking.

✖ Think of the *kind* of information you'd like to elicit from learners prior to asking the questions. For example, you might ask,

> "Does anyone have a personal experience related to this example that might be productive to share with the group? Great, Alex, can you give us a 1-minute synopsis of what happened to you in this situation?"

 # When to Use It

Participant inquiry ought to be used throughout a training session; however, it is especially important to initiate early on in a session as trust and rapport are being established. The technique is also effective for (1) bringing the audience's focus back when they've been distracted, (2) revitalizing a passive group, (3) increasing participation, (4) shedding greater light or perspective on a topic, and (5) determining participants' background or level of exposure to a topic. Skilled facilitators also often use participant responses to transition the group from one topic to the next or to conclude a learning segment.

 # When *Not* to Use It

Participant inquiries, when used too often, can feel contrived and unproductive. It is critical to establish a balance between trainer input and participant responses. It is also important to set time expectations. Participants who don't know when to stop talking can be very disruptive and frustrating. Too little or too much response represents a less than optimal exchange. Be careful not to ask overly engaging questions when time is limited or when you are seeking a specific response. Participant inquiry that is not purposeful and skillfully guided can diffuse the audience's focus, rather than sharpen it.

A Real-Life Training Example

The trainer welcomed participants to the beginning of a weekend workshop. She introduced herself, made a few brief opening remarks, then asked the following series of questions:

> "I'm interested in knowing where some of you traveled from to be here today. Please raise your hand if you're from the local area."

[Some participants raised their hands.]

> "Thank you. Now please raise your hand if you're from within the state of California."

[More participants raised their hands.]

> "Great, now, how many of you have traveled from some where outside the state of California?"

"It's nice to know that we have people here from so many different places. Let's give everyone a hand. Whether you're from near or far, thank you for your efforts in getting here today."

In the above example, the trainer immediately shows interest in her learners. Participants begin to relax and warm up to each other as they find common ground. And most importantly, they unconsciously begin to trust that their trainer cares about them as a person.

Key Concept 10

ADEQUATE RESPONSE TIME

 What It Is

This concept acknowledges that the human brain needs *Adequate Response Time* to shift gears between differing mental tasks such as listening and verbalizing. The best trainers recognize this fact when soliciting learner responses. What is considered adequate time varies from individual to individual and is influenced by the complexity of the information and the learner's prior knowledge. However, a good rule of thumb is to consistently lean towards providing too much (versus too little) time for learners to shift their thinking. When this concept is consistently applied, trainers notice an increase in the quality of group interactions, as well as a wider diversity of respondents.

Although the brain operates at a very rapid pace, it must go through a variety of gyrations, for example, to respond to questions at the conclusion of a lecture. First, it must shift from a passive listening state to one that is conducive to active participation. Second, it must *process* the new information in relation to the question posed. Third, it must generate the appropriate words necessary for verbally expressing the response. And finally, it must deal with the emotional aspects of offering an opinion in public. Simply put, *this process takes time*!

Why It's Important

The downside of asking for responses too quickly is that it may encourage participants with extremely efficient mental processes and/or prior knowledge of the subject to dominate the interaction. Once this pattern is established, it is difficult to undo. Participants who take more

time to process a response may come to believe that they aren't as sharp, despite the fact that they may be making more connections and thinking more critically than the faster responders. As the verbally quick participants dominate the majority of discussions, a counter-productive cycle is reinforced. Since it is the thinking process itself that is most vital to meaningful learning and long-term recall, encourage it!

 # How to Incorporate It

When participants are asked to shift mental gears in the course of a training session, give them sufficient time to mentally prepare. The following activities can help learners practice making smooth transitions from one thinking task to another:

✖ Before asking for questions at the end of a lecture, invite participants to spend 1 minute talking to each other about their reactions to the concept being presented. Then ask them to see if anyone has a specific question concerning the material. Finally, have them thank their partners, face forward, and present their questions.

✖ Break up a lengthy lecture or other passive presentation by asking participants to turn to the person next to them and summarize what they've heard or learned in the past 10 minutes. Give them a specific time frame in which to conclude the exercise.

✖ Give participants 15 minutes to write down anything they want about a topic—thoughts, questions, concerns, or insights—before facilitating a group discussion.

✖ Mentally prepare several different types of questions to elicit supportive responses. For example, if the phrase, "Any comments or questions?" does not elicit a response, have some more pointed and specific questions prepared. Here are a few examples:

- Which parts of this concept need to be clarified?
- How might this principle be applied in your own life?
- How does this lesson relate to the concept we discussed earlier?
- Has anyone used this concept before to solve a problem? If so, how?
- How many of you agree that...? Disagree? Why or why not?

 # When to Use It

The more complex the learning and the less exposure participants have to the topic, the more mental processing time is needed. It is especially important to break up large chunks of learning time with activities that require a mental shift of focus. Invite partner interactions or small group discussions, for example, after a lecture. Or, facilitate a question-and-answer time before asking learners to write about a topic. Break up independent learning activities with group discussions. And remember to give participants adequate time, as well, to make the transition back to listening mode.

 # When *Not* to Use It

Adequate time is a relative term. If the *majority* of participants are ready to respond quickly, less wait time would be appropriate. The key is reading your audience accurately—not just those in the front row or those closest to you, but those at the back of the room, as well. If you notice that a wide variety of learners are volunteering responses and you like the quality of the responses you're getting, you're likely providing adequate time. If, however, the responses don't meet your expectations, try extending the response time.

A Real-Life Training Example

At the end of a 15-minute presentation, a trainer says the classic words, "Any questions?" When this overly used and trite request is answered with the classic blank group stare, she quickly returns to lecturing. At the end of the next segment, she repeats the line, "Now, are there any questions?" She waits a few seconds, looks up at the clock and continues, "Come on, people! Weren't you listening? Don't you care? This is important material! You *must* pay attention!"

At this point, the trainer may have succeeded in intimidating her audience. Even if someone is brave enough at this point to tentatively pose a question, the situation is strained. This result is not what the trainer hoped for, and her chance to generate a lively discussion has passed.

How would you have handled the situation?

The trainer should have realized that the learners' blank stares were quite possibly *external* expressions of a complex *internal* process occurring within the brain. Had she done so, she might have had the patience to guide them through the mental shift necessary to process the information, prepare a response, and articulate their questions.

Key Concept 11

SPECIFY RESPONSE MODE

✔ What It Is

Occasionally, the reluctance of participants to speak up in a group setting, although often multicausal in nature, can be related to confusion about the expected *Response Mode*. Stating *how* you want questions answered is a powerful strategy for establishing a sense of certainty among learners—a fundamental precursor to the facilitation of a lively group discussion.

When our brain is concerned with *how* to respond to an inquiry, our verbal responses may be more hesitant. Our incredible brains are so efficient, however, that we may not even realize what's happening. When uncertainties sift through our unconscious mind, higher-order thinking and verbal communication functions end up taking a back seat to the more immediate concerns of status and appearance. However, when trainers are very specific about how they expect learners to respond, such as saying, "Raise your hand if you're ready to begin," a response is much more likely to follow.

Why It's Important

Participants left to play a guessing game in the training room will digress to basic human operating principles—that is, *no* response is safer than the *wrong* response. When we have to judge what's *right* or *wrong* about *how* we respond, which means facing the possibility of *looking bad*, the desire to respond to a trainer's question can be inhibited. When trainers clearly communicate their expectations, however, the result is a more relaxed environment in which learners feel safe, secure, and certain about what the trainer wants. Once a basic level of trust is established, participants are more likely to involve themselves in the discussion.

 ## How to Incorporate It

It is especially important to use the technique of specifying the response mode in the early stages of a training session when you are establishing a basic level of trust in the room. Once this foundation has been built, you can incorporate more open-ended questions. If interaction starts to wane, throw out a few more invitations for participation. In the following comparison, the questions on the left omit the response mode, while the alternative on the right includes it:

No Specific Response	Imperative
Is everyone ready to begin?	Smile if you're ready to begin.
Have you got the right page?	Nod if you're on page 16.
Did you have a good lunch?	If you had a good lunch, stand up and stretch.
Does this make sense?	If this concept makes sense, give me a thumbs-up.
Who's finished?	If you're finished, look up towards the front of the room.
Does everyone have the handout?	If you've received your handout, hold it up in the air.
Are there any questions?	If you have a question, please raise your hand.

Questions that include a specific direction for how to respond, such as those listed above, help shift learners into the appropriate response mode, which can increase participation. Most questions can be rephrased to specify a response appropriate to your specific context, audience, and topic. For the best results, phrase your questions using positive language and consistently incorporate physical gestures that support the request.

 ## When to Use It

Providing clear expectations right from the start helps foster a sense of safety and supportive risk taking. This technique is also helpful for warming up breakout groups, mixing up modes of participant involvement, involving participants quickly and efficiently, and transitioning from one learning task to another, such as when moving a group from viewing a video to the discussion of it.

 ## When *Not* to Use It

It may not be necessary to continue specifying the desired response after expectations have been established and/or are inherent. Once the pattern of raising hands has been established, for example, you don't need to provide additional prompting unless you wish to shift learners to another mode. Be sure to specify a response mode that is congruent with the type of participants you're training. Specifying a response mode, for example, that carries the potential of embarrassing some individuals (i.e., asking a group of police officers to sit on the floor) could be counterproductive. The role of the trainer, in most circumstances, is to *increase* the comfort level and trust in a group.

A Real-Life Training Example

Participants in a technical writing seminar were at the tail end of a 30-minute writing exercise. The trainer wanted to conclude the exercise and initiate group discussions. He asked participants to spend the next 2 minutes completing the assignment.

The trainer proceeded to busy himself with paperwork, then looked up and said, "Is everyone ready to get into groups?" No one responded, and he noticed that a few participants were still bent over their papers. Immediately recognizing his mistake, he rephrased the question and the response was immediate:

> "We'll begin group discussions in 30 seconds, so please
> finish up your writing at this time." After waiting until
> every one had put down their pens, he said, "Thank you,
> move your chairs into a small circle and wait for the next
> set of instructions."

What happened? Initially, the trainer failed to anticipate what kind of transition would be necessary to move learners from a high-concentration task with an internal focus to one that required an external focus and an inherent understanding of the trainer's response expectation. Some learners were so involved, they didn't even hear the question. When, however, the trainer realized what was happening, he was able to rephrase the question and include clear expectations. Thus, he eliminated the guessing game and replaced paralysis with purpose.

Key Concept 12

PATTERNING INTERACTIONS

 What It Is

Trainers can increase meaningful group dialogue by *Patterning Interactions* in a way that *primes* the brain properly for the task. This technique has an extremely wide range of applications. It consists of the following three components:

1. Ask the question and/or provide the instructions.
2. Provide clarifying details or examples.
3. Repeat the original question or instruction.

Each element in the formula plays an important role. In the first phase, the question or instruction is related to the group in a general sense so that an *overall perspective* is communicated. In the second phase, *details* are given to provide an understanding of the expected responses. Finally, the original question or instruction is *repeated* to serve as a launching point for the discussion. This interaction pattern primes the brain for higher-order thinking, lively dialogue, and a group focus that is clear and productive.

 Why It's Important

The facilitation of a lively and productive group discussion is a valuable tool for teaching adult learners. To be effective, the process requires a skilled trainer. When trainers aren't sure what they want to achieve or are unskilled at engaging participants and keeping them focused, valuable momentum can be lost.

The primary factors that contribute to a productive discussion include (1) a basic understanding of the *topic* to be discussed, (2) a precise under-standing of the trainer's line of *thinking* about the topic, and (3) an understanding of the overall *goal* of the discussion. If participants are kept out of the loop with regard to any of these three factors, the discussion can easily turn unproductive. Thus, patterning interactions into a stan-dard format sets the stage for a stimulating learning environment.

 # How to Incorporate It

Consider the following suggestions:

* When using this technique, include a *rationale* for the assignment. For example, elaborate on how it might impact their personal and/or pro-fessional lives. When the purpose is clear to participants, they are much more likely to invest time and energy in the activity.

* Be sure that the first and third parts of the sequence provide a precise *explanation* of the task and include specific learning objectives. The second part should contain action words, such as identify, list, rank, solve, relate, compare, and contrast, and should help make the learning objectives clear and measurable.

* While it is good to be thorough, it is also important to pattern inter-actions in a concise manner. If you are providing a complex series of instructions, for example, break them down into smaller chunks.

* Before you incorporate this technique into your trainings, it may be useful to practice patterning several different types of instruction sequences (of varying complexity) in a variety of ways. Present the most concise, but still thorough, version.

* To initiate a successful discussion, be sure to repeat the original ques-tion using an emphatic tone of voice and supportive body language. Then continue to guide the discussion as necessary with additional questions.

When to Use It

It is a good idea to follow the patterning formula whenever you are explaining a set of instructions for a group discussion or when initiating an activity in which you want active participation. Although the technique can be used effectively any time, it is especially helpful in the early stages of a session when trainers are seeking to establish a relationship of trust and safety within a group.

 # When *Not* to Use It

It is not necessary to use this technique with instructions that are very short and explicit. For example, if you are using the prior key concept, *Specify Response Mode*, with a simple instruction such as, "When you're done writing, please put down your pen or pencil," no further elaboration is needed. If you can make your point clearly in one sentence, do it!

 ## A Real-Life Training Example

It was during a workshop for staff trainers of a large corporation that I first realized the need for this technique. Ironically, I was conducting a segment on *how to give effective instructions* when I made the connection.

My training plan involved the facilitation of several brief activities with an involved set of directions. After the group completed the activities, I asked them to break into small groups and discuss what they had noticed about the way I had provided the initial instructions. Each group noted comments on a sheet of paper and then picked a spokesperson to read them to the whole group.

The purpose of the follow-up discussion was to increase awareness about the *specifics* of giving effective instructions, such as word choice, length, structure, vocal tonality, and the use of supporting body language. While a few of the comments were related to the

continued...

specifics I had in mind, most were vague and nonproductive, such as, "Your instructions were very good and clear." Since an answer like this does little to move the conversation forward, valuable time was wasted as I tried to gently weed out the misguided comments. Finally, I narrowed the responses down to those that were instructive, but had I been more clear about what I wanted learners to focus on, the exercise would have been much more productive.

Later, I thought about the experience and strategized how I might stimulate a more dynamic discussion next time. I decided I would share the objective of my questioning with the group, rather than expecting them to read my mind. I also realized that I'd been encountering this hurdle at several other points in my workshops.

At that point, I began to use patterning as a way to organize my thoughts to ensure completeness. In the very next workshop, I initiated the same group discussion using this technique:

1. "As trainers I'm sure you all understand the importance of clear and specific directions. When participants understand what you expect of them, your lessons have significantly greater impact. As groups, please use my own instruction delivery as a case study, and consider what aspects of it impacted your understanding, clarity, and follow through."

2. "For example, what did you notice about the words I chose, the tone of my voice, or the gestures I used in leading the activities we have done in this workshop?"

3. "Please discuss in your group what aspects of my instruction impacted your understanding, clarity, and follow through."

This approach—offering a rationale coupled with specific expectations and a reiteration of the initial instruction—has since produced significantly better results.

Key Concept 13

MANAGING DISRUPTIONS

 ## What It Is

Disruptive behavior is an unwelcome guest to the training table. Regardless of age, stage, or setting, there will occasionally be those who seek attention at the expense of others. And yet there's a fine line between seeking attention and contributing. The key, therefore, is to recognize and find a productive way to handle these attention seekers before they have the chance to upstage the trainer. Most of the time these individuals are natural-born leaders whose energy, if channeled properly, can enhance rather than disrupt a training session.

One technique for *Managing Disruptions* is to provide a sanctioned forum whereby participants can share in the spotlight for a time. Interestingly, when attention seekers are recognized and legitimized, the problem usually dissipates. By integrating time for participant humor, sharing, and leadership into your training plan, you not only put an official "stamp of approval" on a*ppropriate* ways to receive attention, you reduce the problem of *inappropriate* responses that divide and disrupt a group.

 ## Why It's Important

It is generally pretty easy to identify a veteran trainer when you observe how they handle these challenging situations. Even when remarks are relatively harmless, it is vital to manage these participants with diplomacy and skill. Your credibility in such moments is either reinforced or diminished.

TrainSmart trainers maintain control of a group with a subtle but strong guiding hand. The most effective way to accomplish this is to provide for learners' attention needs in a trainer-controlled activity that reinforces positive humor, leadership, and participation.

Perhaps the most debilitating form of disruption is *sarcasm*—a Greek word meaning to "tear out the flesh with the teeth." The line between sarcasm and humor can be fuzzy, as well. While good-natured joking and harmless humor can enhance group cohesiveness, sarcasm can alienate participants very quickly. Rather than ignoring sarcastic comments repeatedly, consider how you might bring these inappropriately vocal constituents into the fold. People who are "quick-witted" are often quite intelligent, and if guided correctly, have the potential to make a powerful and positive contribution. Humor that does not rely on stereotypes or poke fun at others can help focus attention, build group cohesion, increase recall, break down resistance, and reduce stress. And it can add an element of joy to an otherwise routine learning task or topic.

 ## How to Incorporate It

Consider the following suggestions for channeling disruptions and fostering humor in the training environment:

✖ Right from the start of any training share with participants how the day/session will proceed, what your expectations are, and how they can actively contribute.

✖ Provide time early on in the training for participants to share something about themselves and/or an opportunity for them to get acquainted with one other and you.

✖ The first time a participant exhibits potentially disruptive behavior, you may wish to ignore it. If it continues more than once, however, initiate an immediate state-change activity. For example, you might transition into small group discussions, if it's appropriate, or facilitate a quick energizer. Disruptions may be a signal that it is time to move on to the next activity.

✻ Provide a "funny-bone forum" in which participants have the opportunity to share a joke or funny observation with the rest of the group. Provide a set of ground rules before initiating this activity (i.e., no disparaging remarks or jokes that rely on stereotyping).

✻ Give groups an opportunity to perform content-related skits or role-plays. Ensure that individuals who like the limelight have an appropriate outlet to showcase their abilities.

✻ Give participants an opportunity to voice any concerns or objections. Sometimes just providing a time to "clear the air" can offset potential problems.

✻ Avoid preaching to or engaging with an argumentative participant. If the remark is relatively harmless, just say, "you might be right" or "I see your point," and move on. Simply acknowledging the individual rather than allowing them to upset you keeps the focus on the training and the task at hand.

✻ Project self-assurance with relaxed but focused body language. Have a plan but remain flexible so that extenuating circumstances can be accommodated with ease. Remain calm and self-possessed when interacting with attention seekers. The goal is to maintain control of the group climate, *not* necessarily individuals.

✻ Use peer pressure to diffuse inappropriate behaviors. For example, if a participant continues to be a problem after you've tried other techniques to productively channel his or her energy, defer to the group. Say, for example, "What do the rest of you think about John's position or opinion on this?" Or ask them, "If you were a trainer and had to handle a heckler, how would you do it?" At the very least, this technique gives you time to strategize your next step.

✻ *Always* confront remarks that hurt others regardless of *who* made them or *why*, *when*, and *how* they were made. Deal with the individual firmly and directly. Ask them to refrain from other offensive remarks in your presence. If that person does not comply, ask them to leave the training.

When to Use It

Although some behaviors or comments may not be distracting to the trainer, they may be to participants. Therefore, it is best *not* to ignore them. There are appropriate times to use subtle techniques and appropriate times to use more direct ones. Consider the situation and the persistence of the problem when making these judgments. Channeling disruptions into appropriate forms and forums is an ongoing process that begins in the early planning stages of a training and continues throughout. Once you have established a respectful and credible command of the group, however, disruptions usually cease to be a problem. Just remember that some personalities are compelled to be in the limelight; respond with appropriate opportunities for everyone to shine.

 # When *Not* to Use It

Do not discourage light-hearted, good-natured humor. There is no better way to break up the tension of an intense learning environment than with a good laugh. Be careful not to be too controlling or overly sensitive; occasionally, even poking fun at yourself can be an extremely effective way to earn respect. In fact, it's not a bad idea to keep a few jokes up your own sleeve for moments that call for it. On the other hand, if someone's remarks are cutting or hurtful, don't use subtle channeling strategies. Instead, ask the person directly and firmly to cease making the remarks. If that person can't comply, ask them to leave.

A Real-Life Training Example

Early on in a staff-development workshop, a trainer realized she had a few sarcastic males in the group and their remarks were getting slightly out of hand. At the earliest opportunity, she asked the audience to form small groups and discuss the following question: What do you think are the most common causes of lost productivity in the workplace? She asked the groups to record their top five reasons. And she added, "Here's the catch: At least one of these reasons *must be sarcastic or funny*!"

As they went to work generating responses, one could hear bursts of laughter erupting from various areas of the room, and a palpable rise in energy was evident. When it came time to give their responses, the trainer asked that they share only the *humorous* ones. When the comedic interlude reached a crescendo, and the participants began to wind down, the trainer said, "Those were great. Thanks. Now, on a more serious note, what other causes of lost productivity did you identify?"

The group could sense a clear shift in expectations. The trainer indirectly, although quite clearly, channeled the sarcasm into an appropriate activity while also setting some parameters to limit its use. The strategy worked: The trainer supported some good-natured humor while also making the group *explicitly* aware that more joking at this point would be inappropriate.

Key Concept 14

CREATIVE NOTE TAKING

✓ What It Is

Absorbing, analyzing, and storing new information in the brain is a complex enterprise—one that is greatly aided by the process of transferring information to paper. Most people recognize that *note taking* is one way to reinforce memory, and many of us depend on this learning tool. But did you know that *Creative Note Taking*—sometimes referred to as mind mapping—further enhances cognition and recall?

Mind mapping (the most common type of creative note taking) is a process whereby learners depict major themes and concepts from the learning with colorful symbols, images, notations, and connecting lines that represent relationships. Creative note taking optimizes learning and recall because it moves us through the process of analyzing information (left-brain function) with a creative emphasis (right-brain function)—thus, encouraging connections across brain hemispheres.

Why It's Important

Traditional note taking can put the brain into "scramble mode" as we try to write down everything we hear. The more hectic this state becomes, and the longer it is sustained, the less time we have to process and thus retain the information. When participants discover, however, that note taking can be accomplished in a more creative and effective fashion, the brain relaxes and learning increases! The images, ideas, or stories that give context and meaning to the trainer's words are what mind maps are made of. These concepts are much easier to remember when associated with symbols, colors, and concrete images. *Drawing notes* in the fashion of mind mapping frees up the brain to pursue other higher-level cognitive functions, such as linking new learning to prior knowledge, recognizing patterns, and critically analyzing information from various perspectives.

 # How to Incorporate It

Give learners a brief overview of the mind-mapping process. Show them a few examples of mind maps or other creative note-taking techniques before starting your presentation.

✱ Supply the appropriate materials: *color* markers or pencils and oversize paper. Consider taking participants through a brief mind-mapping process to clear up any confusion.

✱ Pause often when delivering content. Every 15 minutes, provide a few moments for learners to review their notes and ask questions. During this time, encourage participants to add lines, words, or symbols to their mind maps that clarify and organize their thinking.

✱ Create your own mind map depicting the key concepts related to your presentation and share it with learners early on in the presentation and/or at the conclusion. This provides a valuable overview or road map of the ground you expect to cover and then summarizes it again when you close.

✱ Encourage participants to share their mind maps with each other. The more they discuss their interpretations, the deeper the material will be encoded in their memory. Incorporate small group mind mapping in which the emphasis is on teamwork, or have individuals discuss their respective mind maps in small groups.

✱ Hang participant mind maps around the room and have everyone walk around and view them.

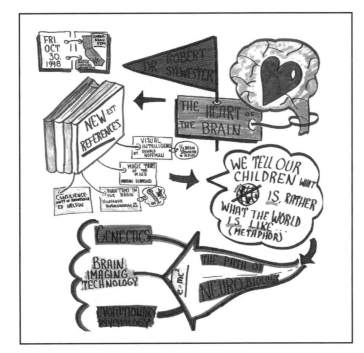

An example of mind-mapped notes on a session called *"The Heart of the Brain."*

When to Use It

It's a good idea to accommodate note taking anytime new content is being presented. Nurture the process by allowing participants adequate time to record the material. And, introduce them to techniques, such as mind mapping, that encourage crossovers between right and left brain hemispheres. Encourage participants to review and clarify material with each other, as well as the trainer(s), during brief but regular breaks.

When *Not* to Use It

Discourage participants from taking notes during activities that involve their active participation or discussion. If you are about to shift from a note-taking mode to one that's more conducive to verbal participation, help participants make the transition by facilitating an informal interaction with a neighbor, a brief break, or a quick movement activity.

A Real-Life Training Example

The setting was a 4-day personal and professional development seminar facilitated extensively throughout the United States, Asia, New Zealand, and Australia. Right from the start the trainer delivered the content with an unusual pattern of speech. He would pause just before the last word of a sentence and wait for participants to complete it (in their minds if not out loud). For example, he might say, "Hopefully it's now clear what I've been trying to...*explain*." He would not actually say the word *explain* until someone in the audience had said it. If no one responded out loud, he would sometimes just continue with the next sentence, never completing the last.

It was a curious approach to content delivery. In a conversation during a break, someone asked the presenter why he did it. He explained that the technique encouraged participants to stay more involved in the learning process. From a theoretical perspective, the idea made some sense. From a personal perspective, however, I confess that I found it mildly irritating—although not enough to significantly impact my experience in general.

Early in the third day, however, I witnessed an occasion in which the approach definitely did *not* work. The trainer had been lecturing about a topic that was of considerable interest to the group—how to make lots of money! At one point, he presented an idea that especially captured the attention of participants. Everyone was furiously scribbling in their workbooks.

At that exact moment, the trainer paused at the end of a sentence, waiting, as usual, for the audience to fill in the blank. This time, however, no one responded. When his pause was greeted with silence, he glared intensely at the audience and said, "Come on, people! You can do better than this! This is important information, and the only way you're going to get it is to stay awake!"

continued...

Strong words, yet I was chuckling inside. As a trainer, he had made a serious miscalculation. He'd failed to recognize *why* people had not responded; they were actively engaged in note taking! In this case, the trainer *interfered* with the learning process by disengaging participants, rather than engaging them. Such miscalculations are not uncommon—even among veteran trainers.

Since the trainer wanted to facilitate interaction, it would have been better to either discourage note taking or allow a transition time for participants to mentally shift gears. A 30-second pause to allow them to complete their notes would have made a dramatic difference in the audience's response.

Key Concept 15

TARGET LANGUAGE

 **What It Is**

Target Language is a communication technique that emphasizes making a request in *positive* terms. It maximizes the chance for a successful interaction between the trainer and the participants. Consider how *you* feel when somebody *tells* you what to do versus *suggesting* a plan. For example, how do you think you might react internally to the directive, "I want you to

introduce yourself to the people sitting next to you"? Compare this with the request, "Let's take a few minutes to introduce ourselves to the others sitting around us." Most adult learners would prefer the second form of communication—especially as the relationship of mutual trust and respect is being established.

A person's most likely internal response to overly aggressive command language, although often unconscious, is to resist the trainer's directions regardless of their potential value. Target language, on the other hand, can open up learning as quickly as aggressive language can shut it down. If you want to empower participants while increasing productive training time, get in the habit of communicating requests in a cooperative fashion using positive terms and diplomatic language.

Why It's Important

When a trainer's words trigger a negative response in participants, critical concentration and focus are lost. Conversely, when a trainer uses positive and cooperative language, they engender a sense of sincerity, trust, and a willingness to follow the trainer's lead—all factors that are essential for successful trainings. Creating a positive environment leaves the participant's mind free to focus on what's truly important—the learning at hand.

 # How to Incorporate It

Carefully crafted language is a powerful vehicle for transporting participants toward the accomplishment of learning objectives. The following specific examples illustrate language choices that can potentially trigger negative responses (labeled "a") versus target language alternatives (labeled "b"), which create a more positive, mutually cooperative feeling.

1-a   *"I want you to find your group and sit down with them."*

1-b   ***"Please find your group and sit down with them, and we'll be able to get started promptly."***

2-a   *"Raise your hand if you've only lived in this state for 2 years or less."*

2-b   ***"If you have lived in this state for more than 2 years, please raise your hand."***

3-a   *"I need all of the teenagers to form a group there, while you adults gather over here."*

3-b   ***"Those of you slightly under 20, please join me in this group, while those of you slightly over 20 join the group near the door."***

Commentary:
In example one, the phrase "*I want you to*" implies a relationship of dominance or power over participants. Dominant communication patterns tend to elicit internal resistance, if not external rebellion, on the part of participants. One of the first lessons most of us learn as children is to use polite

language. Despite this, "please" is still one of the most underused words in the English language.

In example two, the word "only" has a negative connotation. Simply altering the request by dropping the word "only" or rephrasing it in positive terms, makes a world of difference.

In example three, the word "teenagers" is sometimes construed as a negative label, so when the trainer uses it to distinguish or set apart the group, feelings of insecurity, if not threat, may prevail. Many teenagers would rather be adults, while, ironically enough, many adults would prefer to be much younger! The use of the word "slightly," accompanied by a tone of gentle humor in the trainer's voice, should achieve the same result with significantly less potential resistance.

 # When to Use It

Always keep in mind that the objective is to turn learners *on*, not *off*. When we understand *how* our communication choices impact participants, we begin to naturally craft our language throughout a session more sensitively. It is especially important, however, to consciously use target language when using a word to which some participants may be sensitive. It is generally a good idea to be as diplomatic and gentle as possible when first working with a new group. While it may seem overwhelming to do this on a consistent basis, the approach is quickly embodied when trainers experience the positive and productive difference it makes in their training environments. Eventually it will become a valuable addition to your training tool kit.

 # When *Not* to Use It

With the exception of a few hard-core training environments such as boot camp or military school, it is *always* a good idea to use positive and inclusive terms such as *"we," "let's,"* and *"our,"* rather than preachy, dominant directives like, *"You should," "I want you to,"* or *"You need to."* The only time a command using these words is more productive is in the event of an emergency or potentially dangerous situation. If, for example, an unexplained fire alarm sounds, a command like, "Leave your things and file out the back door immediately!" is perfectly appropriate.

A Real-Life Training Example

A visiting principal is organizing a room full of school teachers for breakout discussions. He decides that spreading the newer teachers out among the groups will facilitate the most productive discussions. Thus, he inquires with a smile, "How many of you here are just rookies?"

The principal is quite surprised when his slightly sarcastic comment is not received with much enthusiasm. Rather, he experiences a number of silent stares and mildly hostile facial expressions. Some of the participants even look downright mad. After a few seconds, a bold participant raises her hand and remarks, "How do you define 'rookie'? I've only been a teacher for three years, but I certainly don't feel like a rookie!" The principal realizes his mistake, apologizes, and eventually rephrases his request with more diplomacy. "Please raise your hand if you've just recently begun bringing your talents to the field of education."

In this case, why should the principal single out participants for lack of experience when he has the perfect opportunity to recognize the value they will bring to many students for years to come? The principal's second attempt made many more participants shine with pride, and he avoided making them feel inadequate or under-recognized.

Key Concept 16

INVOLVE, DON'T TELL

 What It Is

Involve, Don't Tell represents a fundamental training principle, one that is surprisingly underutilized in most learning environments. The traditional education model frequently spoon-feeds students—that is, it declares, "This is what you need to know; now repeat (memorize) it." When trainers transmit information this  way, involvement on a deeper level is sacrificed, reducing the chance of critical higher-order thinking through personal processing time. However, when trainers encourage participants to analyze concepts and make connections *through their own mental efforts*, memory increases significantly. Cognitive scientists have proven that when individuals are actively involved in the learning process, information is encoded along multiple memory pathways—physical, mental, and emotional—resulting in significantly better learning and recall.

Why It's Important

When information is transmitted through *involvement*, we are more likely to reflect on the learning and analyze it from various angles, thereby encoding the information more deeply into long-term memory. Active involvement can also increase our heart and respiratory rates—factors that impact our mental and physical energy. Participants who have journeyed actively through a learning process walk away from the session with more than just a hazy cerebral sense of a topic; they take a physical, and likely emotional, memory with them. As such, a solid foundation of meaningfulness and enthusiasm is established, upon which the next level of learning can be applied.

 # How to Incorporate It

The following strategies for facilitating active involvement represent a mere sampling of what's possible. Feel free to expand on them and experiment with your own methods, as well:

✖ Pause regularly and *ask* participants *what they think* the key points are. If the responses you're aiming for aren't provided, facilitate a process of deduction by posing additional pointed questions to guide the group's thinking.

✖ At various intervals during a presentation, break participants into small groups and have them complete a relevant task or exercise. Upon competition, regroup for a debriefing.

✖ Occasionally stop and ask participants to write down any thoughts and/or questions circulating at the moment. Address these issues as soon as possible.

✖ When feasible, give participants the opportunity to learn through experimentation. An immediate hands-on application of new learning increases comprehension and recall.

✖ Performing role-plays, skits, pantomimes, and other theatrical games and creative activities taps into the right-cerebral hemisphere—the area of our brain that synthesizes information.

✱ If you want to ensure recall, "get physical." For example, second-language teachers have discovered that students learn foreign vocabulary better when new words are attached to a consistent movement. Thus, rather than standing at the front of the room and telling students that the way to say jump in Spanish is "brinca," the TrainSmart educator would ask the group to stand and jump in place while practicing the Spanish word for jump.

 When to Use It

Involving participants ought to be the norm, rather than the exception, *throughout* a training. While lectures have a definite place in the training environment, other modes of learning with frequent active involvement will be more successful at reaching the diverse range of learning styles represented in most workshop settings. It is especially important to actively involve participants when they have minimal background and/or experience in the subject or skill set. And, because openings and closings represent critical junctures in the training process, active involvement during these times is especially influential.

 When *Not* to Use It

A fine line exists between presenting *too much* information and *not enough*. Learners clearly need *some* content to put the new learning into context. For example, you certainly can't expect learners to engage in a productive discussion about a subject they know very little about. The key is to find an effective balance between content delivery and active learning.

A Real-Life Training Example

Arizona's Junior Miss was touring her home state giving a series of brief presentations. The topic of her speech was "Domestic Violence in the State of Arizona." At one point during her talk, she threw a question out to the audience: "Did you know that last year 35 percent of women who visited Arizona emergency rooms were there as a result of domestic violence?"

Her primary goal in posing the question was to emphasize and reinforce the most important point of her presentation—the depth of the problem and the lack of awareness about it. But did her delivery maximize the potential *impact* of this important message? She shared a shockingly high statistic: At least, it was shocking to me. Yet, some of its force was lost because the speaker *told* the audience, instead of choosing to involve them in the discovery of it.

In a discussion with her later, we brainstormed ideas for presenting this key fact in a way that would engage the audience more meaningfully and actively. After generating a list of options, she chose the following technique to try at her next presentation:

This time, she asked all participants to raise their hand. Then she posed the following question sequence: "What percentage of women do you think visit Arizona emergency rooms as a result of domestic violence each year? If you think it's 5 percent, go ahead and put your hand down. If you think it's 10 percent, put your hand down." She continued along this line of questioning, increasing the statistic in 5 percent increments. By the time she reached 25 percent, most of the audience had lowered their hand. When she announced that the number was even higher, the effect was dramatic and the audience's physical and mental involvement in the learning process enhanced the possibilities of subsequent recall of this statistic.

Key Concept 17

OWNERSHIP

 What It Is

The concept of *Ownership* refers to the value that participants derive from being included in relevant decision-making processes within the training context. When people feel that their own voice matters, a subtle, yet important, shift in perspective and energy occurs. Trainers use a wide range of strategies to stimulate this shift from *passive receiver to active explorer*. Yet perhaps even more important than techniques that deepen participant involvement is the essential need for trainers to exude an attitude of deep respect for others' experiences and for the collaborative process itself.

When participants are given the opportunity to be involved at the decision-making level, *they no longer sit back and expect the trainer to train them; they become stakeholders in their own success*. This group dynamic not only produces a more stimulating training environment, it balances the onus of responsibility between the trainer and trainees. The popular saying, "If it's going to be, it's up to me," underscores the importance of ownership. Nothing drives progress faster than vesting others in the process.

 Why It's Important

Ownership motivates progress. Commerce has capitalized on this concept for many years; some of the most profitable businesses are employee-owned corporations or companies that offer stock options or profit-sharing incentives. When participants feel empowered, they tend to accept more responsibility for the conditions around them. This shift in perception influences receptivity, and ultimately impacts classroom climate, cognition, and recall. *Meaningfulness* plays a critical role in cognition. When participants get involved and are rewarded for it—both intrinsically and extrinsically—meaningfulness (thus cognition) grows exponentially.

How to Incorporate It

As a trainer you need to emphasize, *in both words and actions*, that everyone plays an important role in the training process. Make it clear that you value the contribution of each person and that the greatest success is achieved in the collaborative setting. The following list represents a tiny fraction of the numerous techniques trainers can use to foster a stronger sense of ownership among participants:

- Have the group create their own list of ground rules at the start of the training.

- Let participants alter seating arrangements as they see fit for the particular exercise or task at hand. For example, rather than saying, "Group A will meet at the back of the room," ask the group to determine *where they would like to meet*. Provide location boundaries if necessary.

- Rather than defining a set of terms for participants, provide a "fill in the blanks" worksheet that offers clues, perhaps like a crossword puzzle. Have participants meet in small groups or teams to complete the exercise; then regroup for a debriefing and answer-sharing session.

- Invite teams or individuals (depending on time constraints) to facilitate a portion of the training. It could be as simple as leading a 2-minute stretch break or as involved as having teams plan and facilitate a complete lesson.

✖ At the beginning of a session, share a schedule outline with participants and ask them if it seems reasonable. Ask them if the break and lunch times are sufficient, if the learning goals are clear, and if they have any questions or concerns. Take into account their issues and, if possible, adjust the schedule to reflect their needs.

✖ Frequently solicit others' viewpoints. If time is a factor (it almost always is), break into small groups so that more people have the opportunity to be heard. Near the end of the training, give participants the opportunity to share their perspective on what was effective and what wasn't. This can be accomplished efficiently through a brief evaluation or feedback form.

 # When to Use It

A sense of ownership needs to be established *early on and then consistently and appropriately reinforced throughout the training*. It may even be appropriate, for example, to let participants decide *how* they will be evaluated at the conclusion of a training. Then provide three options. Providing a narrow list of choices facilitates an efficient process that preserves precious training time.

Once participants are empowered with a sense of ownership, you'll need to continue providing opportunities for them to experience it. While there may be some decisions that are *not* negotiable or appropriate for class involvement, *most* aspects of a training session are or can be.

 # When *Not* to Use It

A trainer, of course, does not need to involve participants in *all* of the decisions that need to be made. In fact, this would practically guarantee a less than optimal training. Advance planning is a prerequisite for success in the learning environment. Many decisions about content, delivery, and the setting itself need to be established long before the day of the training. Determine in advance *what aspects* of the training *are appropriate* for participant involvement, and include participants whenever possible.

A Real-Life Training Example

A trainer walks to the front of the room. She smiles and says,

> "Good morning, my name is Cristal. As we begin, I thought
> it might be appropriate for us to take a few minutes to
> get acquainted with each other. First I'd like to answer any
> questions you may have about my background. Perhaps,
> you're wondering what qualifies me to facilitate this train-
> ing today; or maybe you want to know why I do what I do
> or for how long I've been doing it. I've found that this
> process works best if you write down your questions on
> the index card in your packet. Please take 1 minute to do
> this. When you're done, place your card here on the table.
> I'll address as many of your questions as I can in a 10-
> minute period."

Rather than telling the audience about herself, the trainer has effectively involved the participants in the first process of the workshop.
They now have a vested interest in what happens right at the start of
the day. She has provided very specific instructions, in a tone that is
inclusive and cooperative.

Key Concept 18

PAUSE FOR VISUALS

 What It Is

The concept of *Pausing for Visuals* (e.g., overheads, flip charts, handouts) reflects a basic operating principle of the brain—that is, that it needs a period of time free from competing stimuli to organize incoming visual data. The more novel or complex the material, the more time is needed. The key is to avoid forcing participants to divide their attention between two competing stimuli. For example, have you ever been in a situation in which somebody attempts to explain something to you while you're trying to read about it? The experience is frustrating at best, and frequently counterproductive to learning. A much better alternative is for trainers to respect the fact that the brain may need a moment of quiet contemplation to process new visual information prior to hearing about it.

 Why It's Important

When competing stimuli split a learner's attention, the result may well be distraction, confusion, frustration, or stress. The tendency under such circumstances is to tune out. The learning brain can't possibly pay *full* attention to both elements at once, so it shuts down one or both sensory streams. When trainers, however, respect the brain's basic need for a quiet moment to process new visuals, they not only increase learning enjoyment, they facilitate better comprehension and recall.

How to Incorporate It

If you are in the habit of talking while simultaneously presenting visuals, a period of retraining may be necessary. One way to work around the habit is to explain a concept *before* you post or pass out the supporting material. Since, however, many people are primarily visual learners, it is usually best to pass out or post visuals first and ask learners to study them in silence for a minute or two. While you pause, breath deeply and think S.W.A.E.: Show, Wait, Ask, Explain. This approach may feel awkward at first, but soon it will become automatic. The following tips can support this process:

* Once learners have had a moment to process the new information, *ask* them what they think they do and don't understand. They may surprise you with some very relevant questions. Not only will you have encouraged them to *use* their brain, you will have actively *involved* them in the learning process.

* Provide *additional* processing time when using overheads since many learners feel compelled to take notes or diagram them.

* When appropriate, supply participants with a packet of handouts as they come into the training so that they can review them while waiting for the session to begin.

* Post flip chart pages on the walls around the training room so participants can review them during breaks or between activities.

* Prior to expounding on new visual material, have learners discuss it in pairs or small groups.

* The use of PowerPoint or similar software programs for building visual aids has become increasingly popular. Despite the useful advances in technology, the underlying principles of learning still apply. Each new visual, whether it's a slide, a flip chart page, an overhead, or a computer-generated image, needs to be interspersed with regular and frequent pauses to allow participants sufficient time to process the material.

* How long to pause between visuals is a judgment that you'll have to make moment by moment depending on factors such as complexity of information, learners' experience or background with the subject, and the apparent degree of understanding displayed by participants.

 # When to Use It

Make a habit of *always* pausing for visuals. The length of time will vary, but the practice, itself, should be consistently applied.

 # When *Not* to Use It

A *long* pause may not be necessary when visuals represent a *review* of a topic or when you're displaying uncomplicated images such as photographs. However, even these circumstances warrant a brief pause while the brain reorients itself and registers the image.

A Real-Life Training Example

A corporate trainer presents a series of very impressive PowerPoint images intended to familiarize department heads with a new business model the company is eager to implement. The managers furiously scribble notes while the trainer flips from one viewgraph to the next, supplementing the images with thoughtful explanations. The presentation is flawless, except for one thing. The trainer is completely oblivious to the fact that participants are falling further and further behind. When he finally stops talking long enough to observe the audience, he notices that quite a few people look confused. He realizes they may have some questions. He solicits them, but only one manager responds. Her question clearly illustrates a lack of understanding. This experience reminds the trainer how important it is to provide intermittent pauses between visuals. He decides that at the very next training, he will tape a postcard with the acronym, S.W.A.E on his computer stand to remind him to Show, Wait, Ask, and then Explain!

Key Concept 19

PRESS AND RELEASE

 What It Is

The concept of *Press and Release* reflects the natural ebb and flow between participants' ability to concentrate and their need to relax and mentally refresh themselves. While *press* represents the intense focus required for the acquisition of new information, *release* represents the subsequent "letting go" period that both supports the consolidation of the new material and allows for the diffusion of mental and physical tension. Surprisingly, many trainers underestimate the importance of balancing these distinct mental functions when planning their trainings. Press and release reminds us that both concentration and relaxation periods are critical to the learning process.

 Why It's Important

Press and release creates a dynamic sense of motion in the learning environment. If a careful balance between concentrated study and relaxed consolidation is not maintained, feelings of frustration, exhaustion, boredom, and/or failure are likely to surface. Such feelings, especially when occurring on a regular basis, can hinder learning. Despite the fact that *some* individuals may be able to sustain longer periods of deep concentration, continuous

mental effort is generally *not good* for learning. Under these circumstances we are likely to feel stressed and strained and to eventually fall off-task by daydreaming or "spacing out." The greater risk, however, is that participants may simply choose not to come back to future sessions. Conversely, when trainings reflect a well-balanced schedule of press and release activities, participants not only rate sessions more enthusiastically, they comprehend and remember more.

 ## How to Incorporate It

The following strategies represent both sides of the press and release dynamic:

✖ The more complex or novel the material, the more frequently you'll want to incorporate release activities.

✖ During lengthy press periods, introduce intermittent opportunities for release. Have participants turn to a neighbor, for example, and briefly share what they've gleaned so far from the lesson. Provide guiding questions to keep it simple, quick, and relevant. Perhaps follow up with a large group discussion and address any lingering questions, concerns, or comments.

✖ Mediums such as journal writing, small group discussion, role-playing, mind mapping, games, or art represent productive outlets for both releasing and debriefing after new learning.

✖ Encourage release within work groups by inviting them to include debriefing periods in their team meetings. Suggest a simple question-and-comment period, an acknowledgment activity, or a team ritual.

✖ More effort is required when participants are learning in a language other than their native tongue. In such circumstances, provide additional release activities and offer opportunities to discuss the new learning *in the participant's first language*.

✖ Brief, unstructured breaks provide a natural release opportunity. Energizers or other movement activities also represent viable alternatives.

✖ In a training/learning environment where choice and freedom are provided along with a framework of meaningful structure, mature learners will tend to balance their own press-and-release activities.

✖ Visualization or brainstorming exercises generally constitute a *press* activity as participants concentrate and focus inward. After such exercises, provide a r*elease* by encouraging participants to share their experience in writing or in a small group discussion format.

 # When to Use It

Introduce a release activity of some kind subsequent to any learning session that requires focused concentration. As a general rule for adult learners, break up press periods every 20 minutes with a release activity; however, if you're presenting in a lecture format, if the material is unusually complex or novel, or if participants aren't learning in their native language, provide additional opportunities for release.

 # When *Not* to Use It

Think of press and release as a mutually inclusive dynamic that works like a teeter-totter. It is natural for one end of the teeter-totter to rise while the other falls, but a shift in weight is necessary to restore balance. However, *temporary* imbalances are not necessarily bad: They can induce moderate levels of stress, which actually drive learning and augment retention.

A Real-Life Training Example

Participants were about to start the first phase of an activity challenging them to solve a difficult problem. Although they were organized into small groups, the trainer asked them to consider the problem independently first in silence for 2 minutes before beginning the group-work phase of the exercise. "When I start the music, please consider it a signal to refocus your thoughts here in the room and chat quietly with your group while you wait for my next set of instructions," he explained.

After 2 minutes, the trainer began playing a selection from a Mozart CD and continued writing a series of questions on the chalkboard. While participants waited for their next set of instructions, an air of mystery filled the room and they began talking to each other. Assuming the trainer understood the concept of press and release, what do you think he intended to accomplish during this unexplained pocket of time?

In this case, he had enough experience to know that if he did *not* allow individuals the opportunity to debrief with each other for a few minutes, their attention in the large group discussion would be greatly reduced. Talking informally was the release the trainer knew participants would need after a few minutes of concentrated effort. Thus, he wisely chose to encourage a period of informal exchange and in so doing effectively prepared participants for the next phase of the exercise.

Key Concept 20

PURPOSEFUL BODY LANGUAGE

 What It Is

Our body talks and it speaks louder than our words! Do you know what yours is saying? This is a critical concept in the training environment because the brain registers visual cues such as facial expressions, body movement, eye contact, and hand gestures on a very deep subconscious level. A trainer's body language can either reinforce the information or dis-

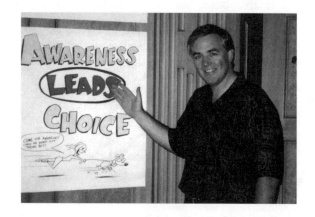

tract participants and interfere with their learning process. *Purposeful Body Language* means supporting the effective delivery of content through the alignment and integration of verbal and physical cues. Training smart means communicating on multiple levels with a well-integrated, believable message.

 Why It's Important

As a general rule, our body language reflects our nonconscious feelings and thoughts. Thus, we can learn a lot about a trainer through careful observation of their gestures and movements. Most of us over the years become quite adept at analyzing both an individual's personality and credibility in this way. We may, in fact, learn as much if not more about people *through our eyes* as we do through our ears. The more honest people are with themselves and others, the more their body language will naturally reflect their verbal message.

 # How to Incorporate It

A trainer's body language, when orchestrated purposefully, can help to maintain learners' attention, facilitate a particular pace, highlight important points, enhance recall, and build trust. It is critical, however, that it be done in a natural, relaxed manner. The following strategies represent just a few of the ways trainers can align their verbal and physical communication styles for an effective delivery:

✱ Watch a videotape recording of yourself and identify which gestures you feel support your message and which ones (if any) negate your message or are not in alignment. Repeat the exercise, only this time, watch a video of a presenter you admire and respect.

✱ Practice your presentation in front of a mirror and experiment with various supportive gestures and facial expressions. Determine which key points you want to emphasize and incorporate a specific technique for achieving this effect at these junctures.

✱ Adjust the *magnitude* of your gestures to reflect the *level* of emphasis you want to achieve. For example, when you deliver the *most* important facts in your presentation, use large body movements, dramatic gestures, and direct eye contact.

✱ Complete stillness can also grab learners' attention and highlight an important point, especially when it is in contrast to your usual movements. Pause for a few seconds, make direct eye contact with the audience, tell them you are about to reveal a key piece of information, and *then* make the point.

✖ Consider your position/location in the room and your posture relative to the type of atmosphere you wish to create. These cues represent significant aspects of communication. If, for example, you're facilitating an intimate activity such as a poetry reading, sit *among* participants on their level, rather than standing over them. If you want participants to listen carefully, stand up front and walk back and forth as appropriate. Pause occasionally to emphasize key concepts.

✖ Rather than holding your fingers up to indicate a first, second, and third element, use broader, more obvious gestures such as the following to clearly distinguish one element from the next: (1) first hold both hands clearly to the left of your body to represent the first element; (2) then hold your hands in front of your body to emphasize the second element; and (3) then hold your hands clearly to the right side of your body while introducing the third element. Another example is to move to three different places in the front of the room while introducing the elements.

✖ When moving from one subject to another, visually demonstrate the transition by shifting your body movements or your position in the room.

 # When to Use It

While it may be impossible to be completely aware of every nuance in your body language all the time, it is quite possible to purposefully incorporate gestures that support your verbal message the majority of the time. This is the goal of using purposeful body language.

 # When *Not* to Use It

Not every word, phrase, or sentence requires an accompanying gesture or movement. In fact, they can easily be overdone. In addition, not every gesture needs to be carefully calculated and precisely timed. Rather, the goal is to *consistently* deliver content that represents alignment in both body and mind, heart and brain.

A Real-Life Training Example

A trainer was addressing the three most important principles of effective communication. She told the participants a story about a manager who had successfully employed these principles in the workplace. While explaining the example, she sat casually on the edge of her desk and assumed a very relaxed posture and conversational tone.

At the story's conclusion, she stood up, walked over to the whiteboard, picked up a marking pen, and in a slightly louder voice said, "Please raise your hand if you recognize any of the communication techniques I've just demonstrated. Let's discuss the impact they made." The responses came fast and furiously. The audience's attention was definitely focused. From the quality of responses she received, the trainer knew that, in fact, the most important parts of her presentation had been clearly demonstrated.

Key Concept **21**

VISUAL-FIELD VARIATIONS

 **What It Is**

A general definition of the *Visual Field* is a person's entire view from a particular vantage point. In the seminar setting, a participant's visual field represents the trainer's "stage"—a stage that is largely underutilized in the typical training environment. How many seminars have you attended, for example, where the norm is stark walls, neat rows of chairs, and a simple podium or table at the front of the room, all of which remain unchanged throughout the session? Maximizing the visual field means attending to the *total* training environment, including walls, bulletin boards, ceilings, windows, manipulatives or props, displays, and peripherals. When trainers judiciously utilize their *entire* teaching and learning stage, the training process is akin to a "surroundsound" experience, and learning is advanced to a whole new level.

Frequent changes in "view point" can help keep a setting fresh and learners' brains alert. Trainers can facilitate visual-field variations by repositioning themselves, repositioning participants, or modifying the room. As trainers, we need to ask (1) Are the walls and display areas full of colorful and relevant images and information? (2) Are the visual aids attractive and easy to read from a distance? (3) Do they reflect the diverse cultures, backgrounds, and lifestyles represented in the group? (4) Are interesting objects, models, and manipulatives placed around the room? (5) How often do they change relative to the content presented? (6) How frequently are participants encouraged to shift their seat or position in the room? And (7) Does the room setup attend to participants' entire visual field?

Why It's Important

Utilizing the full spectrum of a learner's visual field and changing it often represents an extremely powerful tool for creating higher levels of concentration and recall. Visual-field shifts wake up the brain and keep learners alert. Participants naturally shift their range of vision from presenter to others around them, to close-up material, to surrounding displays: As trainers, we need to ask, "What do learners see when these shifts occur?" If they experience interesting, relevant, and novel peripherals, chances are their concentration will remain focused on the learning at hand.

How to Incorporate It

Become more aware of your own visual field shifts and how various training environments impact your conscious, as well as subconscious, mind. This is an ongoing process that will continue to add value to your trainings as your awareness grows. When preparing a training room, walk around and view it from multiple perspectives. Ask the important questions outlined previously and review how you'll incorporate activities such as the ones described below throughout the training session.

✖ It is the tendency of many learners to sit in the same location in a room once they've established it as "theirs." This creates a feeling of comfort for them; however, it can eventually lead to a feeling of stagnation or detachment in a training session. To keep the setting fresh and learners mentally alert, occasionally suggest that participants change their position in the room. Explain the value of doing this and welcome them to find a new seat or move their chair any time they begin to feel bored or distracted.

✖ Facilitate activities that require various room arrangements. For example, have participants move their chairs into a circle for a group discussion or personal sharing. "Circle time" can help break the ice in a new group or support a "check in" or "get acquainted" activity. Consider what participants see while sitting in rows of chairs versus a circle. How does viewing others' faces versus the back of their heads potentially impact learning?

✳ Periodically change the direction from which you are presenting. For example, for a novel twist, ask participants to stand and turn their chairs 180 degrees towards the back of the room. This unexpected request, coupled with the physical effort it entails and the shift in visual field, stimulates anticipation and renewed focus. It's a good idea to have two flip charts available to accommodate such a shift easily.

✳ Place visuals in *every* area of the room so that when learners' attention inevitably shifts, they'll see material *relevant* to the presentation. Hang items from the ceiling, on the door, and on the windows. Pay special attention to bulletin boards and display areas. Provide visually stimulating handouts and make them very accessible. Peripherals of this type support *implicit memory*—a mental process whereby information and images are registered in the brain and encoded without conscious effort.

✳ Use an overhead projection system to highlight key information on an ongoing and easily changeable basis. For example, as participants arrive greet them with a "Welcome" overhead transparency. They'll immediately feel at ease. While you're waiting for everyone to arrive, shift the transparency to one that displays an outline of the proceedings. Before a break, post a transparency that reminds participants when they're expected back and interchange that with a review transparency.

✳ Have participants in small groups or dyads create mind maps and post them on the walls around the room.

✳ In a multiple day training, post photographs on a bulletin board of participants engaged in a variety of learning activities during a previous session.

✳ Provide opportunities for participants to present to the rest of the group from the front of the room or from various places within it. When conducting small group activities, have participants choose someone to record the group's work on a flip chart and then present their conclusions to the large group.

✳ If circumstances allow, utilize the outdoor spaces surrounding the training area. Going outside briefly creates a novel variation in the visual field and refreshes the brain.

When to Use It

Prepare the training room well before the session begins. Place posters and other supporting visuals throughout the room. Plan on implementing visual-field shifts throughout the training session. Many veteran trainers seem to develop a sixth sense about the necessary timing for such shifts. The key is to have a host of visual-field variation strategies at your fingertips to use when you sense the need. Regardless of how interesting or compelling you are as a trainer, learners do inevitably look away. The TrainSmart presenter understands this dynamic and is well prepared for it.

 # When *Not* to Use It

It is sometimes a good idea to *suggest* rather than *direct* participants to make a visual-field shift. And there are times, such as while testing, that a shift would not be appropriate. The goal, of course, is to support, not disrupt, the learning process.

A Real-Life Training Example

A staff-development trainer was well into the third day of a 4-day training when she noticed a lower-than-usual energy level in the room. A number of people looked glassy-eyed and others seemed distracted. She also noted that most participants had continued to sit each day in the same chair. The seating was typical—rows of chairs facing the front of the room.

The trainer decided a visual-field shift might help restore learners' attention, so she offered the following: "Let's take a few minutes to stand, stretch, and breath deeply to re-energize ourselves." After leading a few deep breathing and stretching exercises, the trainer added, "Great...Now, everyone please move their chairs into the center of the room in a large U shape with the top of the U open to the chalkboard."

As the participants rearranged their chairs, the trainer noticed a significant energy shift. Participants were talking to each other, and their faces looked more animated. Once the chairs were moved, the trainer positioned the flip chart at the top of the U. Every person now had a clear view of the presenter, the visual aids, and each other. As she resumed her presentation, the trainer noted that the group's focus had been effectively reclaimed.

Key Concept 22

VOCAL ITALICS

What It Is

Hearing unfamiliar terms can be disconcerting to participants in a fast-paced training environment. Since additional time and mental effort are required to understand new concepts and words, trainers need to determine the background and experience level of participants and adjust their presentations accordingly. Regardless of participants' prior knowledge, however, new learning is supported by (1) *providing time* for participants to comprehend new terms, (2) *emphasizing* new terms with a change in volume and/or vocal tone, and (3) *repeating* new terms verbally several times. This formula is referred to as *Vocal Italics*.

Why It's Important

A trainer's primary goal is simple: We want participants to remember the material we present. Otherwise, why teach it? For learners to understand new concepts and remember them, they need to internalize unfamiliar terms. Accommodating and supporting this process is critical to comprehension. When trainers make a habit of using vocal italics, the brain is alerted to listen more carefully and is supported in the process of learning.

How to Incorporate It

The following examples reflect a combination of vocal italics and related concepts for increased effect:

✱ In the planning stage of your presentation, make a mental or written note of potential unfamiliar terms and concepts. It's a good idea to highlight these words with a bright marking pen in your written outline.

✱ Punctuate new terms with pauses and vocal shifts. For example, the following fact might be italicized this way: "When government hunters in Africa *cull* a herd of elephants, they kill certain members to ultimately benefit the herd. *Culling* is a resource-management practice whereby the size of the herd is balanced with the available *geographic resources*." In this example, the trainer pauses just before and after the italicized words, clearly stresses the pronunciation, and then repeats terms for further emphasis. Here's another example: "This is known as *oxidation*. *Oxidation* is the process by which *oxygen* causes some metals to form rust."

✱ In addition to using vocal italics, monitor your audience carefully for signs of confusion or frustration. If you notice vacant, puzzled, or anxious facial expressions, slow down, repeat new terms and concepts, and facilitate a partner-share or question and answer period.

 # When to Use It

This concept is most critical when the content you're presenting represents unfamiliar territory for your audience. The more prior knowledge your participants have regarding the subject, the faster you can present. It is always a good idea to aim your delivery towards the middle of the experience range, rather than towards the top or bottom. Ask yourself how familiar the *average* participant is with this content. Then proceed accordingly, always adjusting as you go. If participants seem confused, slow down, punctuate new terms and concepts, use terms repeatedly, and then check in with your audience again.

 # When *Not* to Use It

Skilled speakers incorporate vocal italics consistently throughout a session. The key, however, is to match your delivery rate to the average learner's level of understanding. Thus, if you are talking to a group of industry experts on a topic very familiar to them, obviously vocal italics won't be as critical. In general, however, this technique aids comprehension among diverse participants and supports learning.

 # A Real-Life Training Example

A large manufacturing firm held a training on electrical safety for all of its employees. The trainer was an electrical engineer with a graduate degree and many years of experience in the field.

During the presentation, he used terms such as amperes, watts, and volts. Although he provided a brief definition of these and other industry-related words, his delivery was rapid. Some of the employees, many of them nonprofessional level staff, were familiar with the terms, but others had little reason to use them.

Eventually, one dismayed participant raised her hand and said, "Could you please slow down and explain some of the terms you're using? I confess, I'm a little confused at this point and don't understand most of what you're saying."

Several other participants nodded their heads in agreement, alerting the trainer that he'd lost much of his audience. Good-naturedly, he apologized to the group and recapped what he'd presented. This time he slowed down, paused frequently, used vocal inflection, and repeated unfamiliar terms in a variety of contexts. Before proceeding, he facilitated an exercise in which small groups were asked to brainstorm common workplace safety dangers and precautions. During the exercise, he walked around and answered individuals' questions.

The trainer's initial inclination—to direct the training to the highest common denominator (i.e., those participants most experienced with the content) was clearly off base. When, however, he altered his course and employed vocal italics, the trainer effectively reclaimed his audience.

Key Concept 23

MUSIC MATTERS

 ## What It Is

The fact that music can facilitate a state change in our mind/body makes it a potentially powerful tool for trainers. Not only can *Music*, when it is used purposefully, help reduce stress, it can enhance cognition, memory, perceptual-motor skills, and emotional intelligence. We also know that music can induce relaxation, creativity, self-discipline, and motivation.

 ## Why It's Important

Since music has an immediate physical, emotional, and psychological effect on human beings, it can help build social connections, heighten awareness, and provide a sense of safety. It floods the brain in rhythms and beats that induce a wide range of states from energized to relaxed. What better way is there to tap into the emotions and consciousness of a learner than with the music they loved as a youngster or still love?

Effective trainers tap into music's ability to enrich the training environment. At the very least music can enhance motivation, attention, and feelings of vigor. Beyond this, research in recent years suggests it may also improve various brain functions such as spatial-temporal reasoning skills. Other studies suggest that music listening can increase levels of norepinephrine and epinephrine in the brain—two neurotransmitters linked to emotional arousal. While particular music rhythms may stimulate the right hemisphere of the brain (creative thinking, synthesis), other rhythms tend to predominately stimulate the left hemisphere (analytical thinking). Still other researchers note that music's memory- and image-evoking ability stems from its tendency to overlap the auditory cortex with the part of the visual cortex that deals with

visual association. Although this body of science is still young, we can tap into its potential upside benefits with very little downside risk.

 How to Incorporate It

Here are a few easy ways to integrate music into your trainings:

✖ Play an up-tempo selection to energize a group or set a lively mood.

✖ Play a slow-tempo selection to calm a group or set an inspirational mood.

✖ Play nature-inspired music or a Baroque selection to focus participants or to set a mood for concentrated study.

✖ Play music during transitional activities, for example, while participants pick up handouts or reorganize their chairs.

✖ Use a particular song to call a group back from a break or cue participants that the next part of the session is about to begin, much like the theater does when intermission is over.

✖ When choosing a stereo system, consider the parameters of your particular training milieu (i.e., volume requirements, training room acoustics, remote-control feature, load capacity, and ease of use).

✖ Individual preferences regarding music type and volume always vary. Either direct your choices towards the norm or play a variety of selections at varying levels to accommodate the widest range of listeners.

✱ CDs are the most convenient medium for the training environment. Consider buying recordings that represent a *compilation*—reflecting, for example, a certain time period (i.e., the 60's or 80's) or the best of a certain group (i.e., Elton John's "Greatest Hits") or a particular genre (i.e., jazz, classical, hip-hop).

 # When to Use It

The following represent a few choice occasions for using music in the training environment:

✱ *Before a training session begins* (while waiting for participants to arrive), play mood-setting music to encourage friendly exchange among learners. A quiet room can be intimidating and impersonal. Music at the start of a session can also set a positive tone for the rest of the training. Additionally, it provides the opportunity for a clear, nonverbal starting point when it's time to begin: Simply turn the music off to seize the moment *without* having to say, "Ok, it's time to stop talking and direct your attention towards me."

✱ *During transitions or break activities*, energize a group with an upbeat tune.

✱ *During small group discussions*, soft background music without lyrics can "pad" conversations and reduce distractions.

✱ *Close a session* with an inspirational tune that carries a memorable message. Participants will walk away from the training with this as their last impression.

 # When *Not* to Use It

Refrain from playing music, even softly, during testing or content-heavy presentation periods that require intense concentration. At such times, it is best not to introduce any competing stimuli.

A Real-Life Training Example

In a large 1-day workshop for school administrators, participants were divided into two groups. Group A was instructed to meet in the Amber Room, while Group B was directed to meet in the Blue Room. After a logistical briefing, participants were told to take a 5-minute break before joining their respective breakout sessions.

The two seminar rooms were set up exactly the same, except that the Amber Room contained a portable stereo playing upbeat tunes moderately loud. As the group filed in from their break, music sent a wave of positive energy through the room.

The Blue Room, however, had no music, so when participants entered all that could be heard was a dull hum generated by a couple of participants talking quietly among themselves.

The trainer in the Amber Room incorporated music throughout the breakout session, while the Blue Room's trainer did not. Otherwise, the same curriculum was addressed in the two sessions. Two participants in each group were asked to be silent observers—to sit back, observe, and take notes on the group dynamics and degree of involvement.

Participants in the Amber Room bounced in and immediately began talking to others in the room. The trainer used music on and off throughout the session. Participants in the Blue Room, on the other hand, shuffled in and sat down quietly. No music was incorporated.

Afterwards, participants were asked to return to the general session where they were debriefed on the structural differences between the two breakout sessions. The participant observers were asked to share their notes and then the larger group was asked to share its impressions. The differences were striking. Participants in the Amber Room clearly got more out of the session than those in the Blue Room.

Key Concept 24

GUIDING ATTENTION

✔ What It Is

The ability to guide participants' attention effectively may be the single most important underlying objective of any trainer. The key points, no matter how brilliant, will not reach the mark if trainees *tune out*. Equally important is the ability to *recapture* learners' attention after small group exercises, breaks, and/or independent-learning periods. Referred to here as *Guiding Attention*, this concept proposes that trainers can facilitate smooth transitions from one learning task to the next by *inviting learners with verbal and/or nonverbal cues to shift their focus gradually* towards the next activity.

Why It's Important

Guiding attention is a critical aspect of group management. It is particularly important in a highly interactive environment where the training plan calls for frequent shifts, for example, from a lecture presentation to a dyad interaction to a small group activity and so on. While a range of learning modes is highly beneficial to learning, frequent transitions, if not well managed, can disrupt the flow of the workshop.

We know that the brain needs a period of time to transition from one learning activity to the next. This is why it's important to prepare learners for shifts with a stated time expectation, a transition cue or activity, and a brief wrap-up period during which the brain can consolidate and encode new content before moving on. After an activity such as an independent learning task or break, it is best to regain learners' attention by *guiding* it. This can be achieved by emphasizing meaningful relationships between learning activities. Skilled trainers will frequently need to step into the role of facilitators in an interactive learning environment.

 # How to Incorporate It

The following techniques represent just a few of the ways to gain, maintain, and/or regain participants' attention during transition periods.

* When giving instructions for an upcoming learning activity, include a precise time frame and wrap-up cue. For example you might say, "At 5 minutes to 3 p.m., I'll announce that you have 5 more minutes. Please start wrapping up your small group discussions at this time. At 3 p.m., we'll regroup to discuss your conclusions." Note, that a precise time frame was provided as well as a specific cue—the announcement—for initiating the transition.

* Make requests instead of demands. A directive such as, "Okay, everybody, stop talking and look up here now" is jarring and lacks sensitivity to a participant's own learning process. Rather, prepare the group ahead of time, and then ask a question or make a request that is germane to the assignment. For example you might say, "Over the next 30 seconds, as you bring your group discussion to a close, please consider what three elements you personally feel are most important to managing a successful learning organization."

* To regain a group's attention, initially use a voice that is *slightly* louder than the noise level in the room. Then immediately lower your voice, so participants have to pay attention to hear you. The key is to synchronize the momentary break in noise level with a reduction in your own volume.

* Always give participants a "heads up" a few minutes before they need to conclude their present activity. This gives the brain time to prepare for the necessary mental shift. When you use music to alert participants, you avoid having to raise your voice and/or the possibility of being perceived as overbearing.

✖ If you need to unexpectedly gain participants' attention, consider standing on something to make you higher than them. Moving a chair to the middle of the room and standing up on it is one option. Raise your hand above your head and ask participants for their attention. Wait patiently while conversations are wrapped up. As soon as the room is quiet, put your hand down and make your announcement.

✖ Rather than making an abrupt shift to a new topic, bridge the old with the new. For example you could invite participants to share what insights they gleaned from the activity being wrapped up and then briefly relate their responses to the upcoming activity.

 # When to Use It

Guiding attention is a concept that is always relevant. The best trainers never stop facilitating, even when it appears they're not. To be effective, however, we need to plan ahead. In fact, we ought to remain a step ahead of participants at all times.

It is important to incorporate guiding strategies right from the start of a training session. This is the time when participants are most influenced, either positively or negatively. If you don't captivate their attention then, you may continue to have trouble. If you come across as competent right from the start, however, they will be more inclined to follow your lead.

 # When *Not* to Use It

Refrain from bringing closure too soon, especially if the group's energy level is high and they are deeply involved. While such allowances are not always feasible, try to remain flexible throughout a training and don't pack too much content into any one learning session.

A Real-Life Training Example

Participants in a workshop were divided into small groups for a brainstorming activity. They were told they had 30 minutes to complete the exercise, and they would be alerted halfway into the allotted time period. Fifteen minutes into the activity, the trainer was pleased to see that most of the participants were fully engaged in an animated discussion and rapidly jotting down notes.

A few minutes later, a very faint, almost imperceptible level of classical music could be heard. About 5 minutes later, the music became a bit louder, at which point the participants realized they were nearing the closing time. The trainer steadily increased the volume over the next 5 minutes as discussions wound down. Finally, the trainer lowered the volume slightly and said, "Please take the next minute to wrap up. Let's reconvene at five after the hour to discuss your responses."

By steadily increasing the volume of the music, while keeping it appropriate at all times, a smooth transition was experienced by all participants.

Key Concept 25

VERBAL SPECIFICITY

✓ What It Is

The best presenters consistently incorporate the practice of *Verbal Specificity*—a concept that reflects the value of communicating accurate details with precise language to maximize comprehension. Explicit detail helps the brain translate content into concrete, easy-to-grasp images that paint an accurate and intentional picture in the mind's eye. For example, the word "not"—frequently overused by trainers—can conjure up the very image one wants to avoid. To demonstrate, follow this instruction: "Do *not* imagine a huge pink gorilla." The brain, in order to avoid the ludicrous image of a pink gorilla, is actually forced to imagine it. Thus, the result is exactly the opposite of the presenter's intent. This example illustrates the importance of using positive and precise language in the exchange of information.

Why It's Important

When a "learning moment" presents itself, it is important to capitalize on the opportunity. If we fail to engage the learner at this time, we may not have a second chance. Since new learning is often accompanied by feelings of frustration and/or stress anyway, anything we can do to reduce confusion and improve communication is beneficial.

To demonstrate the point, consider that you are going bird watching for the first time. The binoculars you have are old and don't stay focused, so you get frustrated and associate bird watching with work. Now imagine that your first bird watching trip was with an experienced guide who brought along first-rate equipment and a level of expertise that you fully respected. This time you enjoyed the experience, remembered it in detail, and wanted to repeat it. When we're learning something new, clarity and under-standing help keep us on task while reducing frustration and/or confusion.

An important element of verbal speci-ficity is reflected in the following example: A high-school student made a class presentation on the pros and cons of having a computer/Internet station assigned to each student. When she was done, the class clapped and the teacher offered the following acknowledgment: "Well done. Thanks for your excellent effort in putting this very interesting presentation together! Some parts could use improve-ment, but in general it was great!"

This response, although positive, falls short of achieving verbal specifici-ty. While it may bolster the student's confidence, it does little to help her become a more proficient speaker. A response employing the concept of verbal specificity might go something more along these lines: "Excellent presentation, I enjoyed your use of metaphor and the interaction you gen-erated with the audience. I had a hard time seeing your visual aids, however. And I wasn't sure whether I should take notes or if a handout would be provided at the end of your presentation. You might consider these issues for future presentations." The teacher's second response not only acknowledged the learner's areas of strength, it identified ways the student could improve her presentation in the future.

How to Incorporate It

Verbal specificity incorporates a variety of solid communication princi-ples, many of which are reflected in the following recommended strategies:

✖ Use positive rather than negative phrasing whenever possible. For example, replace words such as *can't*, *won't*, *don't*, and *never* with their positive opposites, such as *can*, *will*, *do*, and *always*.

�֍ Avoid using "legalese," "trainerese," or other industry-specific jargon unless you're presenting to an exclusive group in a specific field that understands the terms explicitly. Nothing causes participants to tune out faster than being repeatedly confronted with incomprehensible terms and concepts. As a trainer, it is almost always better to err on the side of using simple, direct, and widely understood language.

✖ Avoid using vague language unless you're doing it for a particular reason. Using exact wording is especially important when providing instructions and feedback.

✖ Add increased meaning to content by using words that paint a mental picture. Incorporate storytelling, metaphor, clarifying examples, and role-playing whenever possible.

✖ Language that perpetuates stereotypes or can potentially disenfranchise certain groups of people (i.e., genders, cultures, religions, socioeconomic class, lifestyle, age, ethnic background, etc.) is never okay. Don't use it and gently correct others if they use it. Be sure that you use both male and female pronouns when referring to people in general. Consider what stereotypes you may be perpetuating yourself and make a conscious effort to avoid this kind of language.

✖ Whenever possible, use a conversational approach, rather than a lecture format or reading from a text. Establish structure in your presentations, but avoid making formal speeches.

✖ Employ all the senses, using colorful and vivid words to describe how an image or scene looks, feels, smells, sounds, and perhaps tastes.

 # When to Use It

Use positively phrased, detailed language whenever possible, and especially when delivering instructions or feedback. Choose words that are positive; paint an accurate mental picture; provide real-life examples. Always respect the power of your words—use it to help participants learn rapidly and easily.

When *Not* to Use It

Of course, there are exceptions. For example, there are times when broad, abstract terms are beneficial. For example, a trainer may want participants to think for themselves in solving a problem or making a connection. In these types of situations, spelling out every detail would probably reduce the benefits of the cognitive process. In addition, the use of negative rather than positive phrasing may occasionally be helpful when highlighting a key point through contrast or comparison.

 ## A Real-Life Training Example

Midway through a training for CPR certification, the instructor distributes a handout that summarizes the key points thus far. He asks participants to spend the next 5 minutes reviewing the handout in preparation for the certification test later in the hour. He provides the following instructions:

"As you review this handout, pay particular attention to the case studies on page two. Be sure to familiarize yourself with the recommended sequence of steps for each type of emergency. The test today will definitely cover this material." With these precise directions, the participants are now more clear about how to prioritize their study time.

Part Three

From Plan
to Applause

Part Three Preview

Six Powerful Parables
1. Animal School
2. The Strawberry
3. The Traveler
4. Two Seeds
5. The 1958 World Series
6. Caterpillars

A TrainSmart Checklist

Six Powerful Parables

When we use analogies, parables, personal stories, and metaphors, we take participants on a vivid and colorful journey that extends the learning to another level. Stories have always been used to convey deep truths and understandings. The Bible—the most comprehensive storybook of all time—makes extensive use of this principle. Perhaps the greatest value of storytelling lies in its ability to involve the listener on multiple levels—engaging our brain, visual system, imagination, and memory. Discerning relevancy through our own mental efforts pays high dividends; thus, story-telling represents a powerful tool for trainers. Whether you use personal examples, fairytales, folktales, poetry, or parables, the skilled storyteller pulls double duty—inspiring as well as teaching.

The parables offered in this section represent some of my favorite training stories collected over the years in encounters with other trainers and trainings. They were shared with me in the spirit of passing on knowledge, and I offer them to you in the same way. Feel free to add them to your own repertoire if they work for you.

1. Animal School

Once upon a time, a community of animals decided to organize a school to meet the demands of their increasingly complex society. Wanting a well-rounded curriculum, they decided each student should take classes in running, climbing, swimming, and flying since these were the basic behaviors represented by most of the animals in the community.

In the first school year, the duck proved to be an excellent swimmer, better, in fact, than the teacher. She was also a very good flyer. However, since she proved less than proficient at running, she was made to stay after school to practice. The duck was even  told to stop swimming to make more time for running. Eventually her webbed feet were so badly damaged, her once excellent swimming technique was reduced to barely passable. Nobody, however, worried—except the duck.

The rabbit started at the top of his class in running, but finally had a nervous breakdown due to his dread of swimming—the subject he could not seem to master.

The squirrel was an excellent climber; however, when the teacher insisted she start flying from the ground instead of the treetops, she developed a psychological block that reduced her to a below-average student.

The eagle was the school's worst discipline problem. In flying and climbing class, he excelled, but he insisted on using his own method to get where he wanted to go. He received an "F."

The gophers ditched school and fought the education tax levies because digging was not included in the curriculum. They apprenticed their children to the badger and later joined the groundhogs to start a private school that offered alternative education.

At the end of the first school year, the animals held a meeting to discuss how their educational system had failed to produce well-rounded learners and successful citizens.

Guiding Question:

✖ How might our own education system(s) be compared to the one reflected in this parable?

2. The Strawberry

One morning a monk was gathering fruit in the jungle when he came upon a tiger. Not wanting to be breakfast for the tiger, the monk ran away. Unfortunately, the tiger pursued. After running hard through the dense foliage, the monk suddenly burst out of the jungle and found himself teetering on the edge of a cliff. With the tiger almost upon him, the monk had little choice but to grab a vine hanging from the cliff top and jump over the edge. The vine held!

Halfway down the cliff, the monk saw another tiger waiting below! As he clung to the vine, trying to decide what to do, a tiny mouse emerged from a hole in the cliff side and began nibbling away at the vine. In this moment of crisis, the monk suddenly noticed a strawberry plant growing from a crevice in the cliff. On it was the biggest, most luscious strawberry he'd ever seen. Temporarily ignoring his plight, the monk reached out, plucked the strawberry, and took a bite. All his fear was suddenly forgotten, for the monk could experience nothing but the intense pleasure of the most succulent, sweetest-tasting fruit he had ever eaten.

Then, just as the mouse finished nibbling through the vine and it fell away, the monk found a tiny ledge to cling to. He held onto it for so long that both tigers became bored and went away. Very slowly, the monk made his way up the cliff, through the jungle, and back to his village.

As he walked, the monk thought to himself: "I learned an important lesson today: Life is precious and time is short. Too often I spend my time worrying about what has happened in the past (tiger at the top of the cliff), what might happen in the future (tiger at the bottom of the cliff), and about the nibbling, nagging problems of each and every day (mouse). With all this worry, I sometimes become blinded to the wonderful gifts life has to offer (strawberry). My fear prevents me from seeing or relishing these gifts. So, not only should we wish for many strawberries (gifts) in our lives, but also for the wisdom to recognize them, pluck them, taste them, and fully enjoy each and every precious bite."

Guiding Questions:

✖ What do you think is the moral of this story?

✖ Could there be more than one moral?

✖ Are there circumstances in your own life that remind you of this story?

3. The Traveler

A traveler was on a long journey. One morning, she noticed her chosen path was becoming increasingly narrow and difficult to navigate. Sensing she may have taken a wrong turn, she decided to ask the next person she encountered if this was the case. She soon entered a clearing and saw a very old man sitting in the center of it. The traveler hurried over to him and said,

"Excuse me, but I was traveling along the path this morning, and it became very narrow. Can you tell me if I'm going the right way?"

The old man answered very softly, "You're on the right path. Keep going. But gather all that you find before crossing the river." The traveler was confused—what did the old gentleman mean by this? But no more of an explanation came from him, so she continued on.

Late in the afternoon, the weary traveler rounded a bend and found herself in front of a river. As she started to wade to the other side, the old man's words echoed in her mind. She paused and looked around, but noticed only trees, shrubs, and pebbles by the river's edge—nothing of any value. Shrugging, she picked up a few rocks, put them in her pocket, and continued across the river.

After reaching the other side of the river, the traveler trudged aimlessly on through dense forest for hours before discovering a new path. She was too tired to go any further and began to prepare a fire. As she knelt down, something hard dug into her thigh and she remembered the pebbles in her pocket. "That old man was crazy," the traveler thought to herself. "I don't know why I've carried these stones around." However, as she cocked her arm to throw them away, a glint of color caught her eye. She looked closer.

"It can't be!" she declared. With the moonlight now shining on the pebbles, the traveler could see that the objects she held were not mere rocks. They were diamonds, rubies, sapphires, and emeralds! The dirt on the stones, she thought, must have rubbed off when she crossed the river. Astonished and dismayed all at the same time, the traveler realized that had she gathered more stones before crossing the river, she'd never have to worry about money again. But there was no going back now: The traveler knew that she would never find her way. At that very moment, she made a vow to herself: From now on, I will always try to see the true nature of something before judging it.

Guiding Questions:

✖ What meaning does this story hold for you?

✖ Have you ever misjudged someone or something?

✖ What happened?

4. Two Seeds

One spring, a young woman planted her garden. Two seeds ended up lying in the ground next to each other. The first seed said to the second one: "Think of how fun this will be! We will send our roots deep down into the soil, and when they're strong, we'll burst from the ground and become beautiful flowers for all the world to see and admire!"

The second seed listened, but was worried. "That sounds nice," he said, "but isn't the ground too cold? I'm frightened to put my roots into it. And what if something goes wrong and I don't turn out very pretty? Then the lady may not like me, I'm afraid."

The first seed, however, was not deterred. He pushed his roots down into the ground and started to grow. When his roots were strong enough, he emerged from the ground as a beautiful flower. The lady tended carefully to him and proudly showed the fragrant blossom to all of her friends, but meanwhile the other seed lay dormant. "Come on," the flower said to his friend every day, "it's warm and wonderful up here in the sunshine!"

The second seed was quite impressed, but remained frightened and only tentatively pushed a root out into the soil. "Ouch," he said. "This ground is still too cold and hard for me! I don't like it. I'd rather stay here in my own shell where I'm safe and comfortable. There's plenty of time to become a flower." Nothing the first seed said changed the second seed's mind.

Then one day when the lady was away, a very hungry bird flew into the garden. It scratched at the ground looking for something to eat. The second seed, lying just below the surface, was terrified of being eaten. But this was his lucky day; just in time, a tomcat jumped from the windowsill and scared the bird away. The seed sighed with relief! And at that very moment he came to an important decision: "It's folly to take my short time here on earth for granted," he said. "I'm going to follow my hopes and dreams for a change instead of my fears." Then without another thought, the second seed began to spread his roots, and he too, grew into a wonderful flower.

Guiding Questions:

- ✖ Do you follow your dreams and hopes or do you follow your fears?
- ✖ Have you ever had an experience in which you had to push through your fears in order to grow?

5. The 1958 World Series

In the 1958 World Series the New York Yankees and the Milwaukee Braves were tied three games each going into the seventh and final game. Warren Spahn was pitching for Milwaukee late in the deciding game. His team was up by one run when the Yankees' star catcher Elston Howard came up to bat.

Milwaukee manager Fred Haney came to the pitcher's mound and told Warren Spahn, "Whatever you do, don't throw it high and outside. If you do, he'll hit it out of the park." Spahn, sending a wet stream of chewing tobacco to the ground, wound up and threw his pitch. It was high and outside. Elston Howard blasted it for a home run, and the Yankees went on to win the game and the World Series, four games to three.

As the Yankees' hero Elston Howard triumphantly rounded the bases, Milwaukee's pitcher threw his mitt down in disgust. He was heard to have said, "Why would a manager ever tell a player what to do by saying what *not* to do?"

Guiding Questions:

✖ What do you think happened here?

✖ Have you ever been in a situation similar to that of the Milwaukee pitcher?

✖ Have you ever told somebody *what* to do by saying what *not* to do?

6. Caterpillars

Processionary caterpillars feed on pine needles. They move in an undulating parade-like fashion across tree limbs, one after another, each connected to the tail of the preceding caterpillar.

Jean-Henri Fabri, a renowned French naturalist, decided to experiment with a group of these caterpillars. Patiently enticing them to the rim of a large flowerpot, he connected the first caterpillar to the last, forming a fuzzy, circular cavalcade with no beginning and no end. He expected the insects to eventually catch onto the joke, tire of the endless march, and start off in some new direction. But not so: Through sheer force of habit, they circled the rim of the pot for seven days and seven nights.

An ample supply of food was close at hand and plainly visible, but it was outside the range of the caterpillars' self-imposed limits. Realizing the creatures would not stop or redirect themselves, even if faced with starvation, Jean-Henri gently broke the chain and led the hungry procession to the nearby food and water.

Guiding Questions:

✖ Why didn't the caterpillars move out of the line and eat?

✖ Did they mistake activity for accomplishment?

✖ Do you think there are any areas in your life where you might be circling like a caterpillar?

A TrainSmart Checklist

When preparing your training plan, the following checklist will help ensure you've covered the key concepts of the TrainSmart approach to perfect trainings every time. It is important to note, of course, that not all of the elements included will be applicable for every training session. Again, the checklist merely represents a framework that requires you to tailor it to your needs. Amend it however you see appropriate.

☐ 1. Do you have a variety of visuals prepared that support your training content?

☐ 2. What will appear on the walls around the training room?

☐ 3. Which areas of the room will be designated for various learning tasks?

☐ 4. What strategies will you implement to put learners at ease and foster lively interaction?

☐ 5. What engagers will you use early in the session to prime participants for learning?

☐ 6. What framing strategies will you incorporate to orient learners?

☐ 7. Have you reviewed and practiced verbalizing your instructions for each activity? Are they succinct, sequential, and clear?

☐ 8. Have you eliminated overly technical terms and provided clear explanations for potentially new ones?

☐ 9. Do the word choices you've made enhance your role as facilitator?

☐ 10. Will you provide participants with a brief explanation of creative note taking techniques?

☐ 11. What strategies do you have planned for creating state changes when needed?

☐ 12. How do you plan to accommodate breaks and/or state-change activities throughout the session?

☐ 13. What strategies will you use to ensure the physical and emotional comfort of participants during group activities?

☐ 14. How will you ensure participants feel empowered? What strategies will you use to instill ownership and personal responsibility?

☐ 15. Does your training schedule incorporate the concept of press and release?

☐ 16. What role will music play during your training?

☐ 17. Have you chosen the music and practiced using the sound equipment available?

☐ 18. What strategies will you use to ensure participants receive sufficient acknowledgment?

☐ 19. In what ways might contrast help highlight the critical points of your presentation?

☐ 20. What strategies will you use to distribute resources efficiently and productively?

☐ 21. What learning activities will you incorporate?

☐ 22. Are your activities followed by a debriefing?

- [ ] 23. At what points in the training will you use open loops? When and how will you close them?

- [ ] 24. What strategies will you use to maintain or recapture participants' attention during transition phases?

- [ ] 25. What thought-provoking questions and clarifying examples will you use to facilitate debriefings and group interaction?

- [ ] 26. Have you included activities that engage the body? What movement activities will be incorporated? Are any of the activities conducted outside or standing?

- [ ] 27. Does your body language and verbal timing support the key points of your presentation?

- [ ] 28. What memory strategies have you incorporated to help participants recall the key concepts?

- [ ] 29. What parables, personal examples, metaphors, or stories will you include?

- [ ] 30. How will you ensure learners have fully understood the content?

- [ ] 31. How do you plan to close the session?

A thorough review of this checklist will not only help you avoid the common pitfalls that trap many trainers, it will assure that participants learn what you want them to learn. Go on and give yourself a round of APPLAUSE!

Education makes us what we are.

—C.-A. Helvetius
Discours xxx
1715-1771

Appendix

BIBLIOGRAPHY

Anderson, J.R. 1990. *Cognitive Psychology and Its Implications*. (3rd Edition). New York, NY: W.H. Freeman and Company.

Bayor, G.W. 1972. *A Treatise on the Mind's Eye: An Empirical Investigation of Visual Mental Imagery*. Doctoral Dissertation, Carnegie-Mellon University. Ann Arbor, Michigan: University Microfilms, 1972. Number 72-12, 699.

Berlyne, D.E. 1965. Curiosity and education. In: *Learning and Educational Process*. J.D. Krumboltz (Ed). Chicago, IL: Rand McNally. 67-89.

Berstein, D. 1994. Tell and show: The merits of classroom demonstrations. *American Psychology Society Observer*. 24: 25-37.

Brigham, F.S.; T.E. Scruggs; M.A. Mastropieri. 1992. Teacher enthusiasm in learning disabilities classrooms: Effects on learning and behavior. *Learning Disability Research and Practice*. 7: 68-73.

Brophy, J.E. 1979. Teacher praise: A functional analysis. *Review of Educational Research*. 51: 5-32.

Burko, H. and R. Elliot. 1997. Hands-on pedagogy versus hands-off accountability. *Phi Delta Kappa*. 80(5): 394-400.

Calvin, W. and G. Ojemann. 1994. *Conversations with Neil's Brain*. Reading, MA: Addison-Wesley Publishing Company.

Campell, J. 1983. *Man and Time*. Boston, MA: Princeton Publishing.

Canfield, J. and M.V. Hanser. 1993. *Chicken Soup for the Soul*. Deerfield Beach, FL: Health Communications, Inc.

Cialdini, R. 1984. *Influence: The New Psychology of Modern Persuasion*. New York: Quill Publishing.

Corey, M.S. and G. Corey. 1997. *Group Process and Practice* (5th Edition). Pacific Grove, CA: Brooks/Cole Publishing.

Cove, P.G. and A.G. Cove. 1996. Enhancing student learning: Intellectual, social, and emotional integration. *ERIC Digest*. (ED400741).

Covington, M.V. 1992. *Making the Grade: A Self-Worth Perspective on Motivation and School Reform*. New York, NY: Holt, Rinelart, & Wisten.

Covington, M.V. and C. Omelich. 1987. I know it cold before the exam: A test of anxiety-blockage hypothesis. *Journal of Educational Psychology*. 79: 393-400.

Cusco, J.B. 1990. Cooperative learning: Why does it work? *Cooperative Learning and College Teaching*. 1(1): 3-8.

Cusco, J.B. 1994. Critical thinking and cooperative learning: A natural marriage. *Cooperative Learning and College Teaching*. 4(2): 2-5.

D'Arcangelo, M. 1998. The brains behind the brains. *Educational Leadership*. 56(3): 20-5.

Dastoor, B. and J. Reed. 1993. Training 101: The psychology of learning. *Training and Development*. 47(60): 17-22.

Driscoll, M.P. 1994. *Psychology of Learning for Instruction*. Needham Heights, MA: Allyn & Bacon.

Evans, G.E. 1988. Metaphors as learning aids in university lectures. *The Journal of Experimental Education*. 56: 98-9.

Fisher, R.P. and R. Geiselman. 1987. *Enhancing Eyewitness Memory with the Cognitive Interview*. Proceedings of the Second International Conference on Practical Aspects of Memory.

Gage, R. and D. Berliner. 1998. *Educational Psychology*. Boston, MA: Houghton Mifflin Co.

Gagne, R.M. and R. Glaser. 1978. Foundations in learning research. In: *Instructional Technology: Foundations*. Gagne, R.M. (Ed). Hillsdale, NJ: Erlbaum.

Glaser, R. 1984. Education and thinking: The role of knowledge. *American Psychologist*. 39: 93-104.

Goleman, D. 1995. *Emotional Intelligence*. New York, NY: Bantam.

Gorman, M.E.; J.A. Plucker; C.M. Callahanj. 1998. Turning students into inventors: Active learning modules for secondary students. *Phi Delta Kappa*. 79(7): 530-5.

Greenco, J.G.; A.M. Collins; L.B. Resnick. 1996. Cognition and learning. In: *Handbook of Educational Psychology*. D. Berliner and R. Calfee (Eds). New York, NY: Macmillan.

Hansen, E.J. 1998. Creating teachable moments...and making them last. *Innovative Higher Education*. 23(1): 7-26.

Hughes, C.A.; J.M. Hendrickson; P.J. Hudson. 1986. The pause procedure: Improving factual recall from lectures by low and high achieving middle school students. *International Journal of Instructional Media*. 13(3): 217-26.

Jensen, E. 1996. *Brain-Based Learning*. San Diego, CA: The Brain Store, Inc.

Johnson, D.W. and F.P. Johnson. 1997. *Joining Together Group Theory and Group Skills*. (6th Edition). Needham Heights, MA: Allyn & Bacon.

Johnson-Laird, P.N. 1988. How is meaning mentally represented? In: *Meaning and Mental Representations*. U. Eco, M. Santambrogio, P. Violi (Eds). Bloomington, IN: Indiana University Press.

Keller, J.M. 1987. Motivational design of instruction. In: *Instructional Design Theories and Models: An Overview of their Current Status*. C.M. Reigeluth (Ed). Hilldale, NJ: Erlbaum.

LaBerge, D.L. 1990. Attention. *Psychological Science*. 1(3): 156-62.

Larkins, A.G.; C.W. McKinney; S. Oldham-Buss; A.C. Gilmore. 1985. Teacher enthusiasm: A critical review. In: *Educational Psychology*. Gage & Berliner (1988). Boston, MA: Houghton Mifflin Company.

Lazar, A.M. 1995. Who is studying in groups and why? Peer collaboration outside the classroom. *College Teaching*. 43(2): 61-5.

Levenson, R.W.; P. Ekman; W.V. Friesen. 1990. Voluntary facial action generates emotion specific autonomous nervous system activity. *Psychophysiology*. 27: 213-5.

Litecky, L.P. 1992. Great teaching, great learning: Classroom climate, innovative methods, and critical thinking. *New Directions for Community Colleges*. 77: 83-90.

Loftus, E. 1992. When a lie becomes memory's truth: Memory distortion after exposure to misinformation. *Psychological Science*. 1: 345-9.

Loftus, E. 1993. The reality of repressed memories. *American Psychologist*. 48(5): 518-37.

Lozanov, G. 1979. *Suggestology and Outlines of Suggestopedia*. New York: Gordon and Breach Publishing.

Maslow, A.H. 1968. *Toward a Psychology of Being*. (2nd Edition). New York: Van Nostrand.

Maslow, A.H. 1970. *Motivation and Personality*. (2nd Edition). New York: Harper and Row.

McConnell, J. 1978. Confessions of a textbook writer. *American Psychologist*. 33(2): 159-69.

Ormond, J.E. 2000. *Educational Psychology*. (3rd Edition). Upper Saddle River, NJ: Prentice-Hall.

Plyshyn, Z.W. 1973. What the mind's eye tells the mind's brain: A critique of mental imagery. *Psychological Bulletin*. 80(1): 1-24.

Poznar. 1995. Goals for higher education from technique to purpose. *Current*. October: 3-7.

Ready, M. 1978. The conduit metaphor: A case of frame conflict in our language about language. In: *Metaphor and Thought*. (2nd Edition). A. Otny (Ed). Cambridge, UK: Cambridge University Press.

Ruhl, K.; C. Hughes; P. Schloss. 1987. Using the pause procedure to enhance lecture recall. *Teacher Education and Special Education*. 10(1): 14-18.

Sapolsky, R.M. 1999. *Why Zebras Don't Get Ulcers*. (4th Edition). New York, NY: W. H. Freeman and Company.

Schacter, D.L. 1990. Impulse activity and the patterning of connections during CNS development. *Neuron*. 5(6): 745-56.

Sfard, A. 1998. On two metaphors for learning and the dangers of choosing just one. *Educational Researcher*. 27(2): 4-13.

Smorginsky, P. 1998. The social construction of data: Methodological problems of investigating learning in the zone of proximal development. *Review of Educational Research*. 65(3): 191-212.

Squire, L.R. 1987. *Memory and brain*. New York: Oxford University Press.

Stepien, W. and S. Gallagher. 1993. Problem-based learning: As authentic as it gets. *Educational Leadership*. 50(7): 25-8.

Sviniki, M.D. 1990. *The Changing Face of College Teaching: New Directions for Teaching and Learning*. San Francisco, CA: Jossey-Bass.

Tomlinson, C.A. and Kalbgleisch. 1998. Teach me, teach my brain: A call for differentiated classrooms. *Educational Leadership*. 56(3): 52-5.

Vergneer, G.W. 1995. Therapeutic applications of humor. *Directions in Mental Health Counseling*. 5(3): 1-11.

Vygotsky, L.S. 1987. *The Collected Work of L.S. Vygotsky*. (Volume 3). R.W. Rieser and A.S. Carlton (Eds). New York: Plen Press.

Weinberger, N.M. 1998. The music in our minds. *Educational Leadership*. November. 56(3): 36-40.

Woolfolk, A. 1998. *Educational Psychology*. (7th Edition). Needham Heights, MA: Allyn and Bacon.

Yerks, R.M. and J.D. Dodson. 1908. The relation of strength stimulus to rapidity of habit formation. *Journal of Comparative Neurology*. 18: 459-82.

SUPPLEMENTAL RESOURCES FROM THE PUBLISHER

Books on Learning, Training, and the Brain

The Brain Store®, Inc., features countless books, posters, CDs, and brain-related products. This innovative education resource company is all about the science of learning. You'll find resources for the following subjects:

- **Teaching and Training**
- **Music and Dance**
- **Enrichment**

- **Organizational Change**
- **Staff Development**
- **Early Childhood**

To view all of our products, log on at **www.thebrainstore.com**, or call (800) 325-4769 or (858) 546-7555 for a FREE color resource catalog.

The LearningBrain Newsletter

Get timely, researched-based articles on a monthly basis. Log on to our online newsletter and stay abreast of the newest and most relevant information on topics like cognition, environment, nutrition, arts, memory, school policy, mind-body, and fragile brains. Save hundreds of hours in research time and expense. Gain twenty-first century teaching and training strategies. To get a free sample issue, log on at **www.learningbrain.com**.

Conference: The Learning Brain Expo®

A world-class gathering featuring more than 45 renowned speakers on the brain and learning. Session topics include music, movement, early childhood, emotions, memory, the fragile brain, and brain imaging. Get dozens of practical teaching ideas and network with like-minded educational professionals. For more information, log on at **www.brainexpo.com**, or call (800) 325-4769 or (858) 546-7555.

Free Samples

Go to **www.thebrainstore.com** to get free tips, tools, and strategies. You'll also find selected products at 40 percent savings. In addition, many books offer you a sneak online preview of the table of contents and sample pages, so you'll know before you order if it's for you. At The Brain Store®, Inc., online shopping is safe, quick, and easy!

Trainings

"Facilitator Training" facilitated by Rich Allen
A 5-day workshop that emphasizes critical training principles and techniques.

"How the Brain Learns" facilitated by Eric Jensen
A 6-day workshop for teachers, trainers, and other change agents with a focus on the brain, how we learn, and how to boost achievement.

"Teaching with the Brain in Mind" facilitated by Eric Jensen
A 3-day program for teachers, special educators, counselors, and other change agents with a focus on what can go wrong with the learner's brain and how to treat it.

For registration information, dates, and costs call (888) 638-7246 or fax (858) 642-0404.

ABOUT THE AUTHOR

Richard Allen, Ph.D., is an international consultant and trainer with more than 20 years experience as an educator. Founder and President of Impact Learning, Inc., he has trained trainers and teachers throughout the world, including the United States, Canada, Hong Kong, England, Australia, New Zealand, and Brazil. Before beginning his educational career as a high-school math and drama teacher, Dr. Allen was an off-Broadway actor. In 1985 he became a lead facilitator for SuperCamp—an accelerated learning program for teens—and has since worked with more than 25,000 students worldwide. At the Pecos River Learning Center in Santa Fe, New Mexico, Dr. Allen facilitated motivational workshops for the top management of such prominent companies as Dupont, AT&T, General Motors, IBM, and Porsche. Dr. Allen completed his doctorate in educational psychology at Arizona State University, where he studied how the human brain receives, processes, and recalls information—knowledge he integrates today into all of his training practices. The author resides in Lake Tahoe, California, and can be reached at his email address: Rich@impactlearn.com.

INDEX

Higher-order thinking 61, 68, 72-3, 82, 90
Humor/comedy 45-6, 52-3, 76-9

I

Icebreakers 4, 36
Inspiration 119, 133
Instructional lane 30
Instructions/directions 21, 31, 43, 47-51, 70-4, 88, 97, 105, 128, 140
Intelligence 65, 77
Interaction/participation 11, 21, 62-4, 67-74, 77, 83-5, 127, 140-2
  (see also Cooperation)
Involve, Don't Tell 90-3
Involvement 10, 20, 90-3, 96-9, 121, 124-5

L

Leadership 76-7, 87

M

Managing Disruptions 76-80
  (see also Disruptions/ distractions)
Meaning 10, 12, 41, 65, 81, 92-5, 104, 123
  (see also Relevancy)
Memory/recall/retention 8, 10, 14-6, 42-8, 56, 65, 77, 81, 90-5, 98, 104, 107, 111-2, 118, 133
Mental effort/involvement 90-3, 102, 115, 133
Metaphors/parables 9, 11-3, 17, 20-2, 127-8, 133, 142 *(see also Stories/story telling)*
Mind mapping 11, 81, 103, 112 *(see also Creative Note taking and Note taking)*
Model 3, 27, 90, 110, 119
  (see also Paradigm)
Mood 20, 45
Motivation 13, 26-8, 52, 56, 118 *(see also Enthusiasm)*

Movement/motion 14, 40, 45-6, 83, 92, 102-3, 106-8, 142
Music 20-2, 45, 57, 105, 118-21, 123-5, 141

N

Norm(s) 34, 45, 92
Note taking 56, 141 *(see also Creative Note taking and Mind mapping)*
Novelty/innovation 15, 52-3, 98, 103, 112

O

Open loop(s) 12, 16-8, 20-1, 142
Ownership 9, 20-2, 94-7, 141 *(see also Empowerment)*

P

Paradigm 3, 7, 139
  (see also Model)
Participant Inquiry 60-3
Patterning Interactions 72-5
Pause for Visuals 98-101
Perceptual-motor skills/ perception 95, 118
Press and Release 102-5, 141
Priming 72

R

Rapport 32
Receptivity 95
Reflection 4-7, 45, 95, 142
Relaxation 102, 118
Relevancy 61, 91, 99, 103, 110-2 *(see also Meaning)*
Repetition 44-6, 72, 115
Resistance 77, 87
Resource Distribution 20, 52-5, 141
Respect 86, 94, 98, 107
Responsibility 9-10, 94-5, 141 *(see also Ownership)*
Rewards 95
Rituals 31, 40-2, 57, 103
Role-plays 7, 11, 78, 91, 103, 129

S

Safety 10, 34-7, 59-61, 69, 74, 117-8, 137
Sarcasm 77-9, 89, 97
Specify Response Mode 68-71, 74
State changes 45, 77, 141
Stereotyping 78, 128
Stories/storytelling 8, 11-2, 15, 128, 133 *(See also Metaphors/parables)*
Stress 36, 77, 98, 103-4, 126 *(see also Anxiety and Threat)*
Stretching 56, 58-59, 95, 114 *(see also Movement)*

T

Target Language 86-9
Task Completion 39-43, 75 *(see also Closure/closings)*
Teach It Standing 56-9
Threat 36-7, 60, 88 *(see also Anxiety & Stress)*
Tone of voice/inflection 46-8, 73-5, 97, 109, 115-7, 123 *(see also Vocal Italics)*
TrainSmart Model 2-19
TrainSmart Schedule 19-20
Transition(s) 31-2, 39, 49-51, 54, 62-5, 69-71, 83-5, 119, 122-5, 142
Trust 35-7, 47, 63, 69-70, 74, 86-7, 107

V

Verbal Specificity 126-8
Visual-Field Variations 110-4
Visualization/imagination 45, 104, 133
Visuals 17, 99, 100-1, 127, 140
Vocal Italics 115-7 *(see also Tone of voice)*

W

Writing/journal writing 103-5